Urbanization in Developing Countries

# Urbanization in the Middle East

Urbanization in Developing Countries

*edited by Kenneth Little*

The first books in the series are:

V.F. Costello: *Urbanization in the Middle East*
J. Gugler and W. Flanagan: *Urbanization and Social Change in West Africa*

Other titles are in active preparation.

# Urbanization
# in the Middle East

V. F. COSTELLO
*Lecturer in Geography, Bristol Polytechnic*

**CAMBRIDGE UNIVERSITY PRESS**

*Cambridge*
*London · New York · Melbourne*

Published by the Syndics of the Cambridge University Press
The Pitt Building, Trumpington Street, Cambridge CB2 1RP
Bentley House, 200 Euston Road, London NW1 2DB
32 East 57th Street, New York, NY 10022, USA
296 Beaconsfield Parade, Middle Park, Melbourne 3206, Australia

First published 1977

Printed in Great Britain by
Redwood Burn Limited
Trowbridge & Esher

*Library of Congress Cataloguing in Publication Data*
Costello, Vincent Francis.
Urbanization in the Middle East.
(Urbanization in developing countries)
Includes bibliographical references and index.
1. Urbanization — Near East. 2. Near East — Social
conditions. I. Title.
HT147.N4C675    301.36'0956    76-11075
ISBN 0-521-21324-X
ISBN 0-521-29110-0 pbk.

# Contents

# Illustrations

# Preface

In his book *The Road to Oxiana* Robert Byron notes as his first impression of Damascus: 'Here is the East in its pristine confusion.' Anyone looking at the field of urbanization in the Middle East might well say the same. There are a number of excellent studies on the Middle Eastern city, mostly collections of scholarly essays but none, I think, attempts to provide a study of the subject from one viewpoint. This I have tried to do in the present work, writing primarily for undergraduates studying social change. In so wide ranging a topic, however, there are inevitable problems of organization, selection and definition.

Foremost among the problems of definition are the terms 'Middle East' and 'urbanization'. The territories grouped here under the title 'Middle East' include Libya, Egypt, the countries of the Arabian Peninsula, Israel, Lebanon, Iraq, Turkey and Iran. The grouping dates only from the Second World War when a single military province stretched from Iran to Tripolitania. As with most regional definitions it is easy to agree on the core area – the Arabian Peninsula, the Levant and Mesopotamia – but it is open to dispute which of the peripheral countries of the region should be included and which excluded. I have included Turkey, Iran, Egypt and Libya because of their intimate geographical links with the core area but I have excluded the rest of North Africa. A distinction between the Middle East and North Africa is increasingly hard to justify, since they have so much in common, but limitations of space preclude consideration of North Africa here; similarly Sudan, which is likely to be treated in a separate volume in the present series. The term 'urbanization' has been used in several ways: urbanization has been described by some authors as an increase in the proportion of a nation's population in urban areas, while an increase in the population of towns, whether faster or slower than the countryside, is called urban growth; others have described the process of an increase in the size of urban settlements as 'urbanization'. In the present work neither of these two definitions will be adopted, since the concern here is both with the demographic event of where people live, and with the social processes involved whereby people acquire material and non-material elements of culture, behaviour patterns and ideas that originate from or are distinctive of the city. To avoid ambiguity, the term 'physical urbanization' will be used to discuss where people live, and 'social urbanization' when questions of social process are involved. I take an 'urban area' to be a settlement with more than 5 000 inhabitants, following the United Nations definition. As we shall see, one of the characteristic features of the Middle East is that there are strong traditions of urbanism, that is traditions of living in towns, as opposed to social urbanization. The social and environmental background to urbanism will therefore be discussed in the first chapter.

To cover so complex a field presents also problems of selection and interpretation. Statistical material on the region is far from comprehensive even now; it is often unreliable and may lack comparability over time and between countries. Published information is available from an extraordinary variety of sources, drawing on work in numerous disciplines, ranging from, say, applied micro-meteorology to social history, each with its own methods, its own assumptions, its own view of the questions one should ask.

What this volume does is to describe how the life of the traditional Middle Eastern city has been transformed by modern physical and social urbanization; in doing so it examines whether the urban ethos developing there is something peculiar to the region, and if that is the case, of what social values, traditional and modern, it is composed. I took as my starting point the idea that urban development is growing from common origins throughout the region towards essentially similar ends, but that one should not lose sight of differences in the social structure of contrasting cities. Accordingly, I included numerous case studies as examples of variations on the general process. But in the course of writing it became apparent that for all the present similarities from one country to another, future, planned urban development may be moving on divergent rather than parallel lines. Added to this familiar difficulty of avoiding on one side too much generality, while on the other the temptation to dwell on the particular, there is a problem in discussing certain social institutions, notably the family and voluntary associations, when there is little material published on them. This, I must confess, may be the result of too heavy a reliance on works published in English. Of these and other shortcomings I am aware, and I trust I will be told of more.

If these were some of the difficulties the task of writing the book was made a great deal easier by generous assistance and helpful comment from many quarters; without them the book could not have been finished. I wish to acknowledge my debt to Kenneth Little, the editor, for a great deal of help given on the broad scope of the book as well as in many painstaking details. Gerald Blake and Brian Beeley read and commented on parts of the manuscript; B.T. Costello read the whole text. Since my days as an undergraduate I have benefited from the fund of knowledge and interest in the Middle East at the University of Durham Department of Geography, and the University of Durham Institute of Middle Eastern and Islamic Studies. I owe much also to my wife Margaret for her forbearance while the book was a-writing.

The book is dedicated, in gratitude, to my parents.

# Acknowledgements

The author and publisher wish to thank the following for
permission to reprint copyright material: the Cambridge
University Press for a passage by H. Bowen-Jones from *The
Cambridge History of Iran*, Volume I, ed. W.B. Fisher,
1968; the Editor, *Town Planning Review*, for a passage from
'The Progress of New Towns in Israel' by Joan Ash, volume
45, no. 4, October 1974; The Department of Geography,
University of Durham, for an extract from *Modern Amman*
by J.M. Hacker, 1960; the Institute of British Geographers
for a figure 'Kashan: Selected Demographic Statistics' in
the article by B.D. Clark and V.F. Costello, in *The Institute
of British Geographers, Transactions*, no. 59, 1973; Jabra-i-
Jabra for three extracts from *Hunters in a Narrow Street*,
1960; Macmillan Publishing Co., Inc., for three passages
from *The Passing of Traditional Society, Modernizing the
Middle East*, by D. Lerner, copyright The Free Press, N.Y.,
1958.

# 1. Environment and society in the Middle East

In so large a region as the Middle East there is naturally great diversity in ways of life and social organization, but there are also common religious, cultural and economic elements making for unity. One common element is Islam, the religion that predominates throughout the region except in Israel and Lebanon. Another unifying element is the Arabic language and Arab nationalism, again with exceptions in the cases of Turkey, Iran and Israel. The oil industry has brought great wealth to some countries while others are among the poorest in the world: in the early 1970s the wealth of states varied from $70 per capita GNP to over $3500. The size of states ranges from 30 sq. km. to 1760 000 sq. km.; their populations from 80 000 to 34 millions (Clarke and Fisher 1972: 18). A further element of diversity has been the amount of Western influence and penetration, varying from attempts at large-scale permanent colonization in Libya and Israel, to Saudi Arabia where European influence has been minimal until recently.

Let us begin by examining the varied physical and social geography of the region. The principal feature of the Middle East's physical geography is a plain of low-lying undulating country running east from North Africa into south west Asia. Three long arms of the sea penetrate this plain, the Mediterranean from the west, the Persian Gulf from the east and the Red Sea from the south. The proximity of these seas to one another and the plain's relative flatness have allowed easy intercommunication between them. To the north, however, is an east—west line of mountains running from the Baltic Peninsula, through Turkey, where they enclose the Anatolian plateau, east to Iran, where they divide to enclose the Iranian plateau. There are other small but locally very important mountain masses: one running north to south through Syria, Lebanon and Israel, and others in the south-western corner and the eastern corner of the Arabian Peninsula. Broadly, the Middle East's climate is divisible into a moist north and a dry south, but with considerable local differences associated with altitude and aspect. Summer temperatures in the south may average 30–35 °C and rise to over 50 °C, but further north and at higher altitude they decrease to an average below 27 °C. Winters in most areas are mild and warm, except at the high altitudes of the Turkish and Iranian uplands, where they are severely cold. Aridity is perhaps the greatest unifying element in the physical geography of the region, in particular reducing levels of population density throughout; yet diversity is introduced by restricted areas of higher water availability where much more intensive agriculture and denser populations are possible, as along the Nile valley and the coastlands of the Black Sea, Caspian Sea and the Mediterranean. Snowmelt on the mountains of the north is an important part of the

[1]

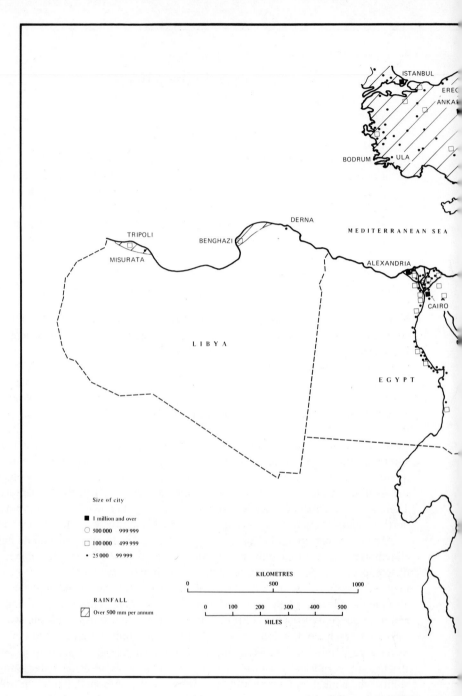

ISTANBUL
EREC
ANKAR

BODRUM    ULA

DERNA

MEDITERRANEAN SEA

TRIPOLI          BENGHAZI

MISURATA

ALEXANDRIA

CAIRO

L I B Y A

E G Y P T

Size of city

■ 1 million and over
◯ 500 000    999 999
☐ 100 000    499 999
• 25 000    99 999

KILOMETRES
0          500          1000

RAINFALL
▨ Over 500 mm per annum

0    100    200    300    400    500
MILES

1. Cities of the Middle East

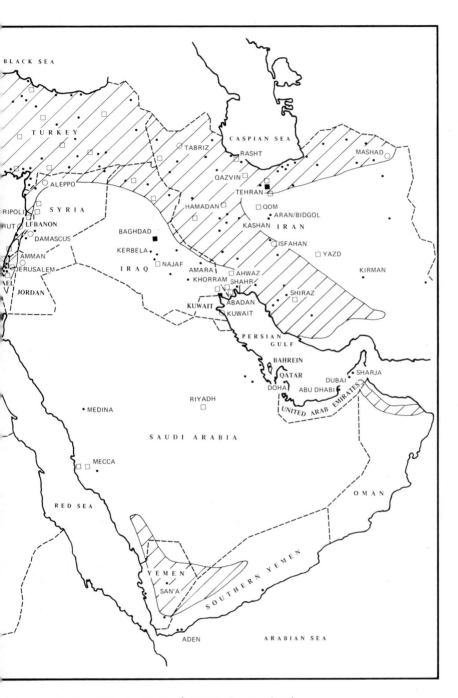

BLACK SEA

TURKEY

CASPIAN SEA

TABRIZ

RASHT

MASHAD

QAZVIN

TEHRAN

ALEPPO

RIPOLI

SYRIA

HAMADAN

QOM

ARAN/BIDGOL

RUT

LEBANON

KASHAN

IRAN

DAMASCUS

BAGHDAD

ISFAHAN

YAZD

KERBELA

AMMAN

NAJAF

KIRMAN

JERUSALEM

AMARA

AHWAZ

AEL

IRAQ

KHORRAM

SHAHR

JORDAN

SHIRAZ

KUWAIT

ABADAN

KUWAIT

PERSIAN

GULF

BAHREIN

QATAR

SHARJA

DUBAI

DOHA

ABU DHABI

RIYADH

UNITED ARAB EMIRATES

MEDINA

SAUDI ARABIA

MECCA

OMAN

RED SEA

YEMEN

SAN'A

SOUTHERN YEMEN

ADEN

ARABIAN SEA

(by permission of the Institute of British Geographers)

water budget in the lowlands of Turkey, Iran and the Fertile Crescent, while rainfall outside the Middle East, in the mountains of Ethiopia, is the major source of water for the settled population of Egypt along the Nile. The human response to this varied environment has been three contrasting, but complimentary, ways of life: nomadism, settled agriculture, and the life of towns.

Nomadism, defined as a way of life involving movement of men and animals in which cultivation plays little part, is of particular significance in the Middle East; less for the number of people directly involved, since this cannot be more than one per cent of the population, than for the imprint of nomadic, especially nomadic Arab, social structures on present sedentary populations. There are two types of nomadic response to the climatic regime of the Middle East, with its winter rains and summer drought: true desert nomads in Syria, Iraq, Egypt and Libya and the Bedouin of the Arabian Peninsula, move into lowland deserts in the winter, return-ing in the summer; while in the mountains of the northern zone nomadic tribes such as the Qashqai of Iran move up to mountain pastures in the summer, returning to the lowlands for winter in a rhythm of movement that is called transhumance. Environmental conditions vary a great deal but in general the more limited the live-stock of a nomadic group, the greater the distances it must travel. Nomadic com-munities are never completely independent in their economy. Animal products are their main source of wealth, but wheat is usually their staple food and this must be acquired through exchange with farming communities. Nomadic pastoralism may in places represent a specialized dynamic response to environmental conditions rather than a decline from a more advanced state of settled life, or the halfway stage between primitive hunting and collecting, and agriculture.

The basic unit of economy is the family household, which enjoys relatively great independence and self sufficiency. The size of social groupings is sharply limited by natural resources in a given district. The next unit above the family household is the tribe, and the more restricted the resources the smaller is the tribal unit. Family relationship within the tribe is strong, maintained by inter-marriage. Control of the life of the tribal community rests on one man, the shaikh, who is the focus of the tribal solidarity and discipline necessary for survival in a harsh environment. The mobility of nomads is usually governed by regulations mutually agreed between tribes, but there is a constant tendency to dispute rights of pasture and occupation, and as a result political combinations larger than the tribe tend, though with some notable exceptions, to be loose and short lived. Some further aspects of tribal society are worth noting at this point: first, hospitality is highly regarded and ordi-nary social intercourse has been elaborated into a very formal code of manners and conduct; next, women in this patriarchal society have low status and are regarded in Arab nomadic society as inferior to men in all things; finally, as a result of frequent invasions and conquests of settled communities by nomads throughout the history of the region, many of the nomads' ways and social characteristics have been carried over into settled life.

One of the names used by Arabic-speaking nomads for settled cultivators was a word that means simply 'cattle', and truly the life of villagers tethered to the land contrasts strongly with the freedom of the nomadic life. Like nomadism, agriculture in the Middle East is controlled by a variety of climatic regimes. It varies from occasional cultivation in even the most arid parts through temporary irrigation by flash flooding to permanent cultivation of intensively irrigated lands in the Nile valley, or on the humid coastlands of the Caspian shore. Because of the strict climatic regime in most parts of the region the management of land and water resources must usually be highly organized and therefore centralized. Whether by village community or by landlord, control of water, the region's scarcest commodity, is vital to agriculture, and there are often disputes regarding the use of water, whether between countries or at the level of the individual.

The allocation of land and water rights follows no single pattern, but in nearly every part of the Middle East agriculture focusses on the village. The village functions as a centre for working the land. Farm holdings are usually scattered in small plots at various distances from the village. Access to the holdings and to water is subject to carefully worked out agreements. Much time may be spent getting from one tiny plot to another and to and from the village. Apart from the natural hazards of drought and disease traditional farming still suffers in many areas from oppressive land tenure systems. Among the most iniquitous was the system whereby landlord and tenant took shares of the crop in proportion to the number of types of input they provided. Thus where the landlord provided land, water, seed, credit and draught animals, and the tenant provided his labour, the landlord took five parts of the crop to the labourer's one. Where the farmer sold his crop or part of it to a market he often found that distance, poor communications and the cost of transportation, plus possible cornering of the market by city merchants, barely left him any better off. Until programmes of Land Reform were introduced by far the greater number of Middle Eastern peasants lived on the extreme margin of subsistence; and so do many still.

The third component in Middle Eastern society is the life of towns. The great variety of geographical environment, with coastal plain, mountain, desert, oasis, steppe and forest, has given a diversity of economic production, and so provided opportunities for exchange and the need for a market centre. The population of the Middle East is distributed very closely in relation to physical resources of water and usable land; the urban population in the past was found in intensively cultivated nuclei, with long stretches of sparsely inhabited or uninhabited land between. Even from the earliest times, however, towns in the region seem to have performed a number of functions in addition to being market centres; they were the focus for religious practices and administration, and appear to have been proportionally more influential in comparison with other regions. A further reason for this influence has been the defence role, significant in maintaining cities such as Aleppo, Ankara and Tabriz, while small groups have often seized power and ruled from an urban base, the Mamluks and Ottomans being good examples, as we shall see in the next chapter.

Furthermore, the major religions of the Middle East, Judaism, Christianity, and

Islam, have close urban associations, with the religious role being the main function of cities like Jerusalem, Mecca, Qom and Kerbela. Cities have also acquired wealth from their hinterlands through absentee landlords, and from time to time the region's position at the cross roads between three continents has helped the development of external city-based trading contacts: west to the Maghreb, by land and sea as far east as China; across the desert or down the East African coast to sub-Saharan Africa; by the Mediterranean Sea or through the Balkans to Europe.

Historically, cities such as Cairo, Istanbul and Baghdad have maintained the widest external contacts and at times their populations were numbered in hundreds of thousands, but their fortunes fluctuated with political and commercial changes. It is these great caravan cities of the Middle East that are best known outside the region. They were not, of course, at any time in the past supplied with the immediate necessities of life, food and drink, by caravan or overseas trade. They relied on their local region for these. The social and economic relations between the city and its surrounding affect considerably the internal social structure of the city. The relations between one city Kirman, and its region will serve as an illustration.

Kirman City was the administrative, social and economic capital of south-east Iran in the early 1960s (English 1966), located in an arid desert basin, of which some 900 sq. km. were permanently inhabited. Because of the scanty rainfall the city depended on an elaborate and extensive system of *qanats* (underground irrigation channels). Qanats are expensive to build and maintain and therefore require large amounts of capital. There are complex regulations about ownership and use. Capital was supplied in the past by wealthy inhabitants of Kirman City, who then controlled the water rights and received a return. The city is the focal point of an organized regional settlement pattern. The oldest settlement, Kirman City, is the largest in the region, at the lowest elevation, and has the widest catchment area for its qanats. Villages in the Kirman Basin may be ranked according to their age, size, elevation and water rights, the newest being smallest and furthest from Kirman City. This hierarchic pattern of settlement is, then, highly organized, and is maintained by continuous communication between its parts. Isolated, self-subsistent village settlements do not exist in the Kirman Basin. A number of other regions on the margins of Iran's arid central plateau showed similar patterns until the recent past (Costello 1976). This is not to say of course that all villages in the Middle East are in the same relation to urban centres as those of the Kirman Basin. Here an urban-based upper-class of officials, landowners, merchants and creditors has maintained its economic and social dominance over the Kirman region through the control of land, water and credit, and through the exercise of political power.

The main function of Kirman and cities like it was as central places engaged in collecting and processing raw materials from the hinterland, and distributing goods, materials and services to the hinterland. However, a purely functional discussion of cities gives only part of the reason for their existence. As well as local environmental relations life in cities is moulded by wider, large-scale social systems. In the Middle East the most significant of these is Islam, the religion of most of the region. It has been argued that Islam has a preference for urban over rural societies, a preference rooted in doctrinal and historical conditions (de Planhol 1968). Islam was born in the seventh century A.D. in the urban and commercial environment of the Hedjaz in west-central Arabia, and it has been argued that its religious goals and rituals are more easily achieved in an urban context. For example, the basic ritual of communal prayer is difficult outside large sedentary communities, and it is not easy to maintain the custom of veiling women in rural or nomadic life. In short, the argument goes, the early Muslims looked on nomads and villagers as merely second-class recruits to Islam, and that attitude has been held ever since.

With their basis of trading activity, administrative control, and religious association Middle Eastern cities have been able to maintain an uninterrupted tradition over millenia, from the earliest urban settlements built by man down to the present day. When rapid urban growth and modern urbanization began in the region one and a half centuries ago, it was on a cultural base peculiar to the region.

# 2. Pre-industrial urban society in the Middle East

The Middle East can claim to have the world's longest history of continuous urban development, but those historical factors which continue to influence urban life in the region date back no further than the Islamic period, following the Arab conquests in the seventh century. When European urbanism was undergoing the so-called Dark Ages which followed the collapse of the Roman Empire of the West, the Arabs were busy founding new towns and regenerating the old Roman towns of Egypt and the Levant, and the Sassanian towns of Persia. The ensuing period of growth and prosperity was the last time when the Middle East led the world in urban culture, and throughout the Middle Ages the urban life of East and West diverged increasingly as each followed an entirely different evolutionary line (Hamdan 1962: 121). The Islamic religion was the principal influence in directing the development of the Middle Eastern Arab and Persian cities of the Middle Ages, though how far and in what ways has been the subject of much debate.

## The Islamic city

When discussing the 'Islamic city' it is necessary to distinguish the variety of functions performed by the city: the functions of the market town, imperial capital, centre of pilgrimage, or military base; to distinguish also their origins: for example the cities created by the Arab conquerors and later dynasties differ from those which were more or less spontaneous; those in the western Islamic world between the Mediterranean and the Arab deserts with a common heritage from Greece, Rome and Byzantium, have a character different from those in the area of Persian culture between the Indian Ocean and the Turkic steppes and deserts (Hourani 1970: 9–10). In addition to such functional and cultural distinctions there are, of course, differences in the character of the Islamic city through time.

    The concern here is to ask whether there were any common features in the Middle Eastern Islamic city and then to ask whether and how these influence the pattern of urban life today. To begin, it will be useful to compare the Islamic city with the medieval European city. Basing his ideas on the European city Weber has suggested that any city can be distinguished by its possession of fortifications, markets, a court administering partly autonomous law, distinctively urban forms of association and at least partial autonomy (Weber 1958: 88). While the pre-industrial Islamic city usually had a market and a wall, it had however no legal privileges and no charter; for Islamic law emphasized that all believers were equal, whether living in town or country; nor did the city have any form of autonomy, any recognition of a distinct territorial status. The multifarious role of the city in Islamic society as a whole has been discussed by Hourani, who points out that the city and the rural hinterland from which it drew its food and to which it sold part of its manufactures may also be analysed as two mutually dependent components of government and society. The countryside needed a ruler, an army and an administration to secure law and order; the town needed a ruler to maintain control over the countryside, and to uphold the laws which allowed a complex urban life. On the other hand the government was able to maintain its administration and supporting army with the taxable wealth produced by the city. In the Islamic period in the Middle East such a relationship was given distinctive shape first by the virtual monopoly of political power for many centuries of politico-military groups, mainly of Turkish origin, who stood a certain distance from the Arabic- or Persian-speaking peoples whom they ruled, and secondly by the close connection between the commercial bourgeoisie and the *ulama* – the class of interpreters of the Koran and the prophetic traditions, and of the laws derived from these two sources (Hourani 1970: 16–18).

The wealth, lineage, piety and culture of the bourgeoisie and the ulama provided them with prestige and patronage. The two groups were often connected by marriage and between them provided some urban leadership, but seldom such as could challenge the power of the ruler. The religious element had no hierarchy or priestly function and by itself could not integrate the elements of the city into a political whole. This was done by the ruler, who stood apart from the rest of society, governing through a group comprising his family, household, palace officials and the army, who were all loyal to his person alone. The ruling group in Egypt even lived in a separate administrative camp, in Cairo, while much of the commercial activity was in nearby Fustat.

Urban society was controlled through a governor and various officials, some responsible for public order, others for justice, while other functionaries supervised public acts of worship. The heads of villages, town quarters, crafts and the non-Muslim communities were each responsible to the government for the maintenance of order and the payment of taxes. The connection between government and subjects could be close, since officials might be drawn from the urban population, and between the ruler and the headmen of communities there were no intervening formal institutions. Indeed, during the Middle Ages, there was in Islam an absence of corporate institutions. Although some features of urban life, notably the baths, the market, the inn, the wall and the gate, had been carried on from the pre-Islamic period, nothing survived of the municipal corporate life of antiquity (Stern 1970: 29). The proliferation of corporations, craft guilds, monastic orders, city councils and other formal institutions is a characteristic peculiar to medieval Western civilization, and the lack of anything comparable is shared by medieval Islam with most other pre-industrial civilizations.

If Islamic law did not recognize the corporation, it did recognize, as a unit between the individual and the whole community of believers, the family as the holder and transmitter of property. The family had the right to live enclosed within its house once the basic necessities of water and sanitation were secured from the community. The individual demanded and secured complete privacy from the city within the family home. There was no sense of corporate identity by the urban population as a whole, and the great open spaces, piazzas and gardens of the cities, were the result only of the largely self-interested generosity of the ruling groups, or of some sense of community on the part of religious leaders (Scanlon 1970: 182).

The physical form of the Islamic city partly reflected its social structure, though the variety of functions performed by different cities, together with variations in site, climate, local building materials, and a multiplicity of cultural and temporal differences gave each city its own shape and personality. Some cities had an overall plan, imposed by some ruler at some time, but within this framework the residential areas were a jumble of twisting alleyways, with the occasional open square used as market, a recreation ground, or the scene for such events as public executions and public funerals. There were however a number of features common to most cities.

First, there was the seat of military power, the citadel, placed usually on a natural defensive site, and in many cases, like Khorramabad in Iran, surviving almost intact today. Next, in the larger cities there was a royal palace, home of the ruler and his numerous entourage, which might form a separate quarter. The royal quarter might be quite separate, as Cairo was from Old Cairo (Fustat), or it might be an enclave in an existing urban agglomeration, as the Topkapi palace was in Istanbul. Summer palaces were sometimes outside the walls, as at Fin near Kashan. A third major feature was the complex of institutions and buildings associated with the central mosque and the bazaar. The principal mosque functioned as a place of prayer, a court of justice and an intellectual and educational centre, and it might also be a place for secular activities such as eating, drinking and recreation (Ismail 1972: 117). The principal mosque had a dome and a minaret, and was usually the tallest structure in the city. Associated with the mosque were religious schools and monastic establishments. Apart from the mosque and the royal household where the administration was carried out, there were no official buildings accessible to the public. The court of the judge or the governor was architecturally indistinguishable from the bourgeois house (Graber 1970: 213). Close by the mosque might be a hospital, since medicine was an important branch of learning, together with public baths and latrines, the latter adopted from the Roman and Byzantine urban traditions. The bath house was a place of informal social contact, where ritual and hygienic cleansing was done, together with massage. In the privacy of the bath house women could meet in groups to discuss their own affairs.

Commercial premises were found in all cities, but their size and the range of goods and services offered varied with the size and function of the city. The bazaar, or *suq*, was a market usually covered for protection against the elements. Inside the bazaar complex were shops, numerous shrines, and in the larger commercial centres *khans*, or *caravanserais*, designed for the meeting of merchants and the storage of goods. The khans consisted of a courtyard, sometimes roofed, around which were rows of stores and offices, the whole protected by strong gates. Retail shops must have been similar to those of today, small and crowded, lining the walls of the bazaar. A medieval illustration of a shop selling milk and dates shows it simply as a small opening cut out of a wall (Graber 1970: 213).

Finally, a feature common to Islamic cities in the Middle East was the type of house. In Persian and Arab lands the basic residential unit was a house built on several storeys around a central courtyard, often with a pond. It faced inward, away from the hurly-burly of public life. The form of the house resulted from the demands of climate, of family life and of Islamic ideology. Much of the Middle East has high temperatures during the summer daytime, but the nights are cool. High desiccating winds are common. These climatic problems were solved in the traditional house by a number of adaptations. Various parts of the house suited different times of the day and year. Rooms opened into the courtyard and windows on the exterior walls of the houses were lacking or of minimal size, and the high narrow shape of the court restricted insolation. During summer nights when everyone slept on the roof, cool air forming on the flat roof sank into the courtyard; during the day radiation from the protected courtyard surface helped cool the house (Dunham 1960). Illumination without gloom or glare was provided by protective lattice work over the windows (Ismail 1972: 115–16).

The emphasis on family privacy meant that if possible visitors were segregated. Male friends and callers were received in the public rooms, while the private rooms, the *haram*, remained a family sanctuary. To effect this the house might be divided into upper and lower storeys, the visitors using only the lower storeys, or there might be a separate court for the haram. The size of the courts was kept within strict limits, because only a small courtyard can be protected from the sun. A large urban family might therefore live in several conjoined courtyards. Poorer families could not afford a building divisible into public and private rooms and did not receive many visitors.

We have seen that the Islamic cities of the Middle East share common features in their ideology, the structure of society and of government, and in their physical form. In detail government and ways of life did of course vary, and we shall examine examples of different types of city, showing what was peculiar to each but how each was a variation of the same general pattern. Two illustrations will be taken from the Middle Ages, after which period internal decay in Islamic society and the assaults of Europe from the outside initiated changes in ways of life away from the traditional model though, as our third illustration will show, the general forms of Islamic urban life continued in many places until the present century.

Much of our information about the pre-industrial Islamic cities of the Middle East comes from sources relating mainly to large cities. Data on the smaller cities come mostly from archaeological work, which attempts to piece together a picture of urban life and society from buildings and artifacts, as at Siraf on the Gulf (Whitehouse 1972). It is difficult to infer the nature of social organization purely from the physical facilities and forms associated with it; accordingly we shall take as examples cities for which the studies published have used written sources.

## The Middle Ages

A comprehensive portrait of urban society during the period A.D. 969 to 1250 has been given by S.D. Goiten, using the documents of the Cairo Geniza. In this Geniza (a room for discarded writings) from the tenth to the nineteenth centuries, middle-class Jews deposited their letters, court records, business accounts and literature, believing that writings on which the name of God might be found should be buried, like the human body, rather than destroyed.

During the period 970 to 1250 in particular, under the rule of the Fatimids, the cities of the eastern Mediterranean flourished in an environment which allowed widespread international commerce and freedom of communication. Urban society during the period was characterized by a considerable degree of commercial free enterprise and religious tolerance. Cairo was governed by a military commander, who was assisted by a superintendent of police and the city judge who had substantial judicial and administrative functions. The city was subdivided into a number of areas each with a superintendent. There were nightwatchmen and regular and mounted police to maintain order on such occasions as that when a fight broke out between rival groups in a synagogue (Goitein 1969: 91). Independent of the city judge were the secret police, the 'informants', who were of special importance in activities against subversive politico-religious groups.

The links between Cairo and its immediate rural hinterland were maintained by personal contact. Many people of modest means, as well as the rich, owned and personally administered farming land. Olive growing, sheep breeding, viticulture and associated industries were all carried on, but the rough work was done by peasants. There may have been some urban antipathy towards living in rural areas, and in one instance referred to by Goitein a Jewish woman said she would not go with her husband to a particular community in the countryside (1967: 76; 1969: 96). The greatest of medieval Muslim historians, Ibn Khaldun, lumped together the peasantry of the fields and the nomads of the desert as 'outsiders'; marriage between townsmen and peasant women was not considered feasible.

There are only two social layers referred to in the Geniza documents: the upper class of business men or bankers and the lower-class manual workers. Government servants and religious scholars did not form a well-defined social class (Goitein 1967: 75). This gross division into upper and lower class conceals many different strata, of which the people mirrored in the documents were definitely conscious. The upper class, the bourgeoisie of businessmen and professionals, itself divided into two. The lower group contained the master artisans and was referred to as 'beggars' by their more exalted fellow citizens. This class could be divided into the urban craftsmen and labourers and, at the bottom, peasants and those in unclean occupations.

A man's place in society was assigned by his origin, since the father's occupation was usually followed by the son, but also his religiosity and learnedness were important, since to be a fervent believer in and a gifted expounder of his creed, whether

Islam or Judaism, was highly honourable. Other factors enhancing the social status of an individual and his family were integrity and sound business practices and a reputation for liberal public spending. Natural gifts or good luck enabled a man to move into a higher class, and no doubt the reverse also happened. Some occupations, such as those of cleaners of sewers and cesspools, street cleaners and bathhouse attendants, were generally despised. On one occasion, during a period of strife between the ruling oligarchy in the Jewish community and the rank and file some of the latter were contemptuously labelled as performing low grade manual occupations such as those of oyster gatherers, dyers, potters and cobblers (Goitein 1967: 91–2). Because it was too similar to slavery, wage earning was a degrading occupation, so individuals preferred to enter into some sort of partnership in their business dealings if at all possible.

Women did a great deal of the work, not only the domestic chores but in crafts also. The small scale of industrial enterprises allowed much work to be carried on in the home. There were many female professions, such as bridecombers (specialists in assisting at the bride's preparations for her wedding), doctors and dressmakers, but no respectable women were engaged rumuneratively in domestic help. This work was performed by female slaves, an important section of the working population. In fact one modern scholar argues it was the presence of female slaves in the haram that contributed in part to the deterioration of the status of free urban women from the tenth to the nineteenth centuries (Baer 1964: 34). Male slaves in Cairo in the Fatimid period were engaged for the most part in finance and commerce (Goitein 1967: 147).

Christians and Jews living under Islam during this period formed communities of their own, centred on the synagogue or church. They shared language, economy and most of their social habits with their Muslim compatriots, but in communal life they were left mainly to themselves. The free exercise of their religion and the administration of their own affairs was left to them so long as they paid the poll tax and submitted to certain restrictions. Their life, honour and property were safeguarded. In effect they formed a state beyond the state, since they owed loyalty to the heads and the central bodies of their own denominations. Law was personal rather than territorial, and an individual was judged according to the law of the denomination to which he belonged, not according to where he found himself, though criminal law remained the preserve of the state. Education and the numerous works of charity such as the care of widows and orphans and the ransoming of captives were provided by the community. One of the many personal details which emerge from the Geniza documents is quoted by Goitein: in a letter of thanks from a Jewish proselyte to a woman who fed him in hard times, he gives her instructions on how to bake fine cakes, not forgetting an injunction to put hot ginger in them (1971: 407, 129). The religious communities were vigorously democratic in structure up to the mid-thirteenth century when military feudalism and a narrow Muslim clericalism were imposed on the whole of society (Goitein 1971: 1–5).

Fustat was closely built up, with at least half the lanes and alleyways being dead ends. No mention is made of public open spaces, but there were cattle pens and places for spreading things, presumably for drying cloth, just as the flat roofs of traditional houses are used today. There were promenades and parks outside the city perimeter and, judging from allusion in the documents, numerous private gardens. There is no evidence, apparently, for compulsory zoning of the city, but divisions did exist, with many names of bazaars, streets and squares indicating specialism in a certain trade or industry. The divisions were not rigid: Jews, Christians and Muslims could live in adjacent houses, a performer might live in a street of cobblers, and a judge in a druggists' bazaar. Houses were readily convertible into workshops and no doubt much industrial production like spinning and weaving was carried out in private households. A feature of the city was the abundance of ruins, which were much remarked on, as they were by Europeans in the nineteenth century. The ruins resulted from the practice of common partnership in houses and the consequent neglect of their upkeep, together with the high cost of trained labour, which made repairs expensive, though rents were low. The mixture of land uses in the city did not mean that there were no variations in land values. Analysis of the price of property in Fustat indicates that the city was divided into neighbourhoods of houses of higher and lower value (Goitein 1969: 86–97). Although it is generally held that pre-industrial cities had few variations in land values (Sjoberg 1960) the evidence from Fustat is further indication that a mixture of residential and industrial land uses could exist in the pre-industrial city together with a recognizable land value surface (Costello 1973).

In the years after 1250 until the early sixteenth century, Syria, Palestine and Egypt were ruled by the Mamluks, a state of slave soldiers which maintained itself by constantly importing men from distant countries to occupy military and key administrative roles. The freedom of commerce and international communication which had obtained under the Fatimids was replaced by a more oppressive regime. Seaports were dismantled or destroyed and the coast laid waste to discourage attacks by European navies, which continued even after Acre, the last Crusader stronghold on the mainland, fell in 1299.

The social structure and political organization of Damascus and Aleppo in the later Middle Ages under the Mamluks has been discussed at length by I.M. Lapidus (1967). The Mamluk state was run as a national military system, with a slave caste of soldiers atop the rest of society. Beneath the military elite were two other broad classes: the local bourgeoisie together with the religiously learned, and the common people who may be divided into, on the one hand, working people such as craftsmen and shopkeepers and those with some social respectability, and on the other hand, the poor, the vagabonds, those in despised and unclean occupations. The respectable working people and the outcasts were organized into communities associated with quarters in the city. These residential quarters were at some remove from the central mosques and bazaars and had their own markets, bathhouses and other facilities. Lists compiled in the sixteenth century gave Damascus seventy quarters and a further thirty in the suburb of al-Salihiyyah, with about fifty quarters in Aleppo (Lapidus 1967: 85). Size varied, but a population of the order of a thousand per quarter was probably typical.

The solidarity of the neighbourhoods was based in some cases on religious identity. Jews, Christians and others lived in groups, while among Muslims ethnic groups, Arabs, Kurds and others lived separately. Among the Arab Muslim majority affiliation to one of the schools of law, clan ties, or a common village origin might draw people together into a quarter. In general communities were made up of rich and poor, though to some degree some quarters were richer, others poorer. The quarter performed specific functions in the Mamluk city. It formed an administrative collectivity and was supervised by a shaikh, who was chosen by Mamluk governors of the city, and who acted as spokesman for the community. The quarter was responsible for the apprehension of criminals, and the shaikh performed some police functions. The quarter formed a single unit for taxation, the rates of tax being negotiated with the government by the shaikh. In times of danger and unrest the quarters organized their own defence, setting up barricades and gates, and in extremes, later in Ottoman times, were even walled off from one another. They were not, however, isolated ghettos, but adjacent streets and districts of the city.

So intense was neighbourhood communal solidarity that at times faction fights broke out between quarters. Such hostilities might be deliberately fomented by the Mamluks for their own ends. These feuds in Damascus and Aleppo were centred mainly on quarters outside the city walls, and the name of some factions was derived from tribal origins, indicating that some groups did not lose their fierce tribal loyalties on settling in the city. The movement of rural peoples to the city was of greater volume in the unsettled later years of the Mamluk regime and under its successor, the Ottoman State. This movement resulted in urban groups which preserved the habits of social organization more appropriate to nomadic than settled life (Lapidus 1970: 199).

The strong communal ties in the quarters, coupled with an absence of independent corporate economic associations, produced a society where economic grievances could seldom be articulated without group violence. Political communication with the ruling foreign caste was limited. Food shortages or abusive taxation provoked street demonstrations, assaults on officials, pillage of shops and the closure of markets. Although disturbances might rise to the level of city-wide rebellion each was aimed at a particular end, the removal of an especially vicious governor, or a reduction in taxes. The communities would unite to such ends but were too parochial in membership to encompass the destruction of the form of government, or even to conceive of political revolution. Furthermore, the religious, the ulama, maintained and preached that loyalty to the good order of society transcended all else.

There were other forms of associational life, the fraternal societies, of which the two most important identified by Lapidus were the young men's gangs (*zuar*), and the Sufi orders. The zuar in Damascus were uniformed, self-consciously organized bands of young men led by recognised chiefs. They were organized by quarters, which they defended at times by fighting pitched battles against the Mamluks. At other times their pursuit of self-interest led them to act as auxiliaries for the Mamluks, being armed and paid by them to repress nomad or village violence and to extort money from the city population. As organized racketeers they preyed upon the quarters, running protection rackets, pillaging and murdering. The Sufi orders, the other form of fraternal association, were bands of religious mystics who lived a communal life under their own shaikhs and teachers. There is a great assortment of such orders in Islam (Levy 1962: 89–90). A debased form of Sufism was found in a group called the *harafish*, the beggars, who belonged to dervish orders and who lived on the charity of the Mamluk Sultan or at working in the more menial occupations in society. Like the zuar, they were occasionally used by the Mamluks in civil wars, seizing such opportunities to pillage where possible (Lapidus 1970: 200–3).

The fragmentation of cities into small communities living in discrete quarters and plagued by violence from criminal gangs conveys a picture of disorder and insecurity. Muslim urban society in the late Middle Ages did however partly cohere around common acceptance of Islamic values, elaborated and preserved by the ulama, and around a diffuse acceptance of the various schools of Islamic law. The regulation of family life, commercial transactions and education was carried out by the ulama, the religious, professional, commercial and managerial elite all in one. They could act as spokesmen for the people. The management of defence and taxation in the absence of a city-wide community organization had to be given to the Mamluks. Lapidus concludes that the domination of foreign rulers in the Arab world during and after the Middle Ages had its basis in an order of society in which towns like Damascus and Aleppo could not fully govern themselves (1969: 205).

The division of the city into numerous village-like quarters has further implications, since there was no discernible social, geographical or ecological quality which made the cities single communities. Socially, the loyalties of city people were attached less to the city than to their immediate neighbourhood community, which might be identified with one of the four major orthodox schools of religious law. Frequently the majority if not the whole population of a district formed by a market town and its surrounding villages shared adherence to a school of law. Where the city was divided between several schools or sects corresponding religious groups were often found in the countryside; and in Rey in the twelfth century communal warfare among sects involved surrounding villages. Such ties between village and city were strengthened by economic and social bonds between urban and village families; where there was rural antagonism it tended to be part of a wider economic, social or religious antagonism.

The cities were dependent on their regional hinterlands for support, but with regard to function they had no unique characteristics. The facilities associated with urban areas such as fortifications, marketing facilities, Sufi convents and principal mosques could be found, and are found today, in villages. The size of a settlement's population is an unreliable indicator of importance, partly because most accounts were estimates and often liable to exaggeration, and the cities themselves were often composite settlements. Isfahan was a composite settlement: in it Jay and the Jewish settlement of Yahudiya were separate entities in the tenth century and in the sixteenth century Armenian Julfa was added on the other side of the Sefid Rud river (Lockhart 1939: 14). The Islamic notion of a city was, then, diffuse.

**Urban decline**

In the late fifteenth and early sixteenth centuries two significant forces began to affect the nature of Islamic urban society in the Middle East. The first was the expansion of the Ottoman Empire. After the conquest of Asia Minor and the destruction of the Byzantine Empire in the mid fifteenth century the Ottoman Turks eradicated all traces of pre-Islamic non-Turkish urban life in Anatolia. They next overthrew the Mamluks and expanded their dominion over nearly the whole of the Middle East with the exception of Persia and of lands they disputed with the Persian Empire. Under the Ottomans the urban craft guilds which had existed in Islam for some time acquired a strongly religious background. The citizen craft guilds consisted of a rigid hierarchy of masters, journeymen or master apprentices, and ordinary apprentices. The guild regulated the quality and quantity of a particular good manufactured and sold in the city. The initiative allowed to members was small: the number of shops was limited for each guild and only master craftsmen were allowed to open shops; no changes in fashion were allowed without the guild's sanction; and the price of the commodity was fixed by the government (Gibb & Bowen 1950: 281–3).

Far from being the independent corporations that are associated with the name of 'guild' in Western Europe, these organizations were developed under the protection of the government as an instrument for the effective control of the state's population and economy. They were mostly small bodies of craftsmen, though they did range in size from over 12 000 down to the guild of torture-instrument makers with just one member (Baer 1970: 28–50). The Iranian guilds appear to have been similar in function to those of the Ottoman Empire. They grew out of bodies of craftsmen engaged in the same occupation that were created by the government for fiscal and administrative purposes. The guilds in Iran were the only urban economic body to be taxed as a unit and they chose their own chief and officers (Floor 1975: 101–2). On occasion guilds participated in religious ceremonies and there were often tea houses in the bazaar frequented by one guild, but their social and political role was of little significance. Their fiscal and administrative roles were assigned to them by the state; any other roles they might acquire were of minor importance.

While the Ottoman Empire was expanding so too was maritime Europe. Symbolically enough, at the same time in the early sixteenth century as the Portuguese were assaulting the world of Islam from the outside by creating havoc in the trade with the East, the first European penetrated to the heart of the Islamic world by secretly entering Mecca and Medina and returned to publicize his travels (Saunders 1966: 115).

The achievements of Islamic urban civilization in the political, military, intellectual and artistic fields were already well past their peak by the early sixteenth century, yet on the eve of Europe's expansion the Islamic world was convinced that it had nothing to learn from the barbarian West. The causes of the decline in urban civilization, which continued despite the physical expansion of the Ottoman Empire, were multiple and are still matters of historical speculation. Even by the Middle Ages urban populations are thought to have declined from Roman times, hastened by the destruction wrought by periodic invasions from Central Asia.

The population of Baghdad in the sixteenth century was about 50—100 000, perhaps a tenth of its former maximum. Egypt's total population in the eighteenth century was about two and a half million, having fallen from a figure of not more than four million in the fourteenth century. The populations of Syria, Iraq and Arabia likewise decreased. The cultivated area in the Middle East shrank, irrigation works fell into disuse in many areas and trade declined. It is thought that urban life probably suffered less than rural, but the quantity and quality of handicrafts declined. Though seventeenth-century Alexandria, Tripoli, Aleppo and Baghdad were still important commercial centres European competition and the stagnation of their hinterlands steadily reduced trade to a trickle (Issawi 1966: 3—4; Hershlag 1964: 7—8).

Among the economic factors contributing to the general decline was the exhaustion of timber resources. Wood is the most important material in pre-industrial societies for the construction of artifacts, from houses to ships, to ploughs, and it is a principal source of fuel. The deforestation of much of the Middle East's uplands over millenia, with subsequent overgrazing, led to severe soil erosion throughout the region. Since the natural ecological balance in arid and semi-arid areas is particularly delicate and easily upset, regeneration of woodland has been and will be a hard task.

Nor was the structure of Middle Eastern society conducive to change, partly because in the course of repelling a succession of invaders — Crusaders, Mongols, Turks — the Arab countries had transformed themselves into militaristic 'feudal' societies. The political and military power of the Ottoman Empire was steadily weakened by constant warfare, while the economy of the Empire suffered from the inflationary effects of South American gold coming in from Europe. Central authority in the Empire began to break down in the seventeenth century; nomads increased their depradations on settled communities, and there emerged a number of local petty dynasties and quasi-independent governors. A broadly similar course was followed by the Persian Empire, with occasional expansion and contraction but with a bloody and destructive invasion by the Afghans in the eighteenth century, until a period of internal consolidation and reform under the Qajar dynasty in the nineteenth century.

The scientific and intellectual life of Islamic society in the Middle East had likewise been in decline since the Middle Ages. Religious authority became greater and more restrictive, shown in one instance by the persistent attempt by religious leaders to maintain a ban on tobacco, although there was no Koranic evidence to support their views. The Ottoman government was finally obliged by public pressure to lift the bans and only then in 1725 could the tobacco sellers form themselves into a reputable and accountable guild (Gibb & Bowen 1950: 292). It was not until the early eighteenth century that the despised infidel printing press was allowed into the Empire. Commerce became increasingly concentrated in the hands of non-Muslim minorities who were not subject to the rigours of Islamic law. The non-Muslims were formed into communities called *millets* and were permitted to organize their own religious, social and legal lives. These groups were concentrated in the major commercial centres of the Empire. Later, their existence gave a ready-made excuse for the Western powers to interfere in the Ottoman Empire's internal affairs.

## Kirman City

A description of one city, Kirman, around 1900 is given by P.W. English in his study of settlement and economy in the Kirman Basin (1966: 39–45). It is of interest here because the general lineaments of urban structure and organization in Kirman as late as 1900 were similar to those of other Iranian cities of similar size and, in this comparatively small market city, outside the bounds of the Ottoman Empire, the general forms of Islamic urban life were similar in a number of ways to those of the Middle Ages. In many details, such as the presence of craft guilds and their functions, they were similar to those of the Ottoman Empire.

The central mosque, the citadel and the bazaar were the three institutions which formed the core of Kirman City. Dating from the fourteenth century the central (Friday) mosque was the Kirmanis' main place of communal prayer. Close by were a number of bathhouses where religious ablutions could be performed. The walled citadel near the western city wall sheltered the homes of the city's political and commercial elite. The commercial district, called the Vakil Bazaar, lay between mosque and citadel. The main section of the bazaar ran for some 600 metres; it contained covered stalls, caravanserais and alleyways where most of the city's trading was done. After the typical Persian pattern, the Vakil Bazaar was linear, with each trade or craft located in one section. The jewellers, cloth sellers, coppersmiths and other retailers were located around the bazaar's two major squares. All the important wholesalers however, whose trade did not require them to be on a thoroughfare, were found in the caravanserais which had multi-storied open courtyards with storerooms and offices cooled by wind towers. These towers are tall square structures designed to catch any cooling wind and direct it to the rooms below. They were an important architectural feature of Iran's desert cities, as were domed water cisterns which were fed by conduits running under the city alleyways.

The four Muslim residential districts inside Kirman's walls had the usual twisting alleyways, arches and dead ends, and were just wide enough for two donkeys to pass. The mud-brick courtyard houses were divided where possible into public and private rooms. The blank outside walls could hide the fountains, columns, stained glass and elaborate plaster ornamentation of a rich carpet nabob's house, or a drab and humble dwelling where the womenfolk laboured all day at a carpet loom. The houses in Kirman's Jewish quarter were well protected from intrusion by high walls and massive doors; the facilities necessary to Jewish social and religious life, baths, schools, a butcher shop and two synagogues were located at the heart of the quarter. The Zoroastrian quarter was outside the city walls, remote from the centre of commercial and social activity. Zoroastrians were under a number of restrictions with regard to dress, taxes and other matters, and by law their houses had to be low enough for a passing Muslim to touch the roof. The community was governed by a council of social and religious elders. The district was noted for being the cleanest and most orderly part of Kirman.

The structure of society among Kirman's Muslim majority was based on a clear division separating the owners of land, water rights, credit, and carpet contracts, who constituted the upper class, from the commoners. There was little movement between classes. Among the lower class there were few income variations, apart from the despised social groups of beggars, prostitutes, bath attendants and others. The extended family of man, wife, unmarried children, married sons and relatives is thought by English to have been the fundamental social unit among the wealthy and to a lesser extent among the poor, who had little economic means or incentive to hold together large family organizations. Commercial transactions in Kirman were regulated by product guilds, as they were in the Ottoman Empire. The solidarity of bazaar and other workers was aided by their membership of a *zorkhaneh* (house of strength), a club for traditional Persian athletics.

Outside the family religion was the principal unifying force in nineteenth-century Kirman. The ulama wielded economic power through the administration of religious endowments and spiritual influence through the control of education, preaching and the religious courts. Religious values and practice were stressed in the elementary school, and the menfolk especially came together for religious occasions, the most notable being the annual performance of passion plays in the month of Muharram to mourn the martyrdom of Imam Hussein. Kirman, like most of Iran and part of Iraq, is of the *Shia* sect of Islam, a sect which regards Ali as the first Imam or successor of Muhammad and rejects the first three *Sunni*, that is orthodox, Caliphs, following Muhammad. The Shia sect does not accept as authoritative the traditionary part of Islamic law, based on Muhammad's reported words or acts, but not written by him. The Shia passion plays are a keynote in Shia life, and since the Imam Hussein was killed by orthodox Muslims, they serve among other purposes, to emphasize the rejection of orthodox Islam.

The total population of Kirman remained stable at about 40 000 souls; and stability, concludes English, was the dominant feature of social patterns in nineteenth-century Kirman, with little migration into or out of the city and little social mobility (1966: 99–101). Certainly in comparison with the changes which had overtaken Egyptian urban society by 1900 this small, sleepy market town had remained untouched by the more vigorous upheavals of the nineteenth century.

A person's life in the pre-industrial Middle Eastern city centred on his family, kin, religion and means of earning a living. The importance of family and kinship groups is common to most pre-industrial urban civilizations, and common to many was grouping of population by sect or tribe rather than social class; but it was religion that gave the Middle Eastern city its distinctive stamp, affecting as it did family and personal relations, the physical form of the city, its mode of government and political structure. Even the manner in which commercial transactions were carried out was governed by a religious code of ethics. The importance attached to family and tribe may also be traced back to the tribal nomadic influence on Middle Eastern society, with patterns of life formed in the desert or steppes being carried over into the settled life of city and village.

Each of these aspects of traditional urban life will be dealt with in subsequent chapters which study how they have changed and how they influence urban life today. From the sixteenth century onwards, however, the wider commercial and political world in which the Middle Eastern city existed began profoundly to be altered. At first it was the long-distance trading contacts of the large caravan cities that were affected by the expansion of European power. For over three centuries these wider contacts suffered from a progressive atrophy, though the relations between cities and their immediate hinterlands probably did not alter a great deal. The market, administrative, pilgrimage and local strategic functions of most cities remained. During the nineteenth century, however, the function of many Middle Eastern cities began radically to change as European commercial enterprise, supported by the demands of a growing industrial revolution, began to look to urban hinterlands as well as the cities. Later in the Middle East, as will be seen in the next chapter, the flag followed trade.

When the economic structure of the city and the state changed so also did the social structure, accompanied by an agonised reappraisal of society by Middle Eastern thinkers and leaders in the face of what was apparently a reversal of the divinely ordered nature of things. The following chapter will show how the Middle Eastern city was drawn into a wider, non-Islamic system of politico-economic relations, and investigate some of the social effects of the resulting change in urban process.

# 3. Modern urban development

The purpose of this chapter is to examine the chief factors responsible for the transition in ways of life and urban process from the Islamic pre-industrial city to the modern city. The transformation got under way during the nineteenth century. It came not as a natural development of late medieval society, but rather through an alien European invasion, initially through trade but later, in places, through direct military action. Egypt was the first to be invaded — by Napoleon in 1798 — and Egypt was the earliest country to be pushed towards integration with the new world economy. Other countries were not invaded by European armies until the twentieth century; the period of direct colonial rule in Libya was less than thirty years, and some countries maintained nominal independence throughout. During the present century, however, all the states of the Middle East have actively encouraged the import of Western technology and institutions in their efforts to modernize the state and the city. As the commercial, industrial and technical climate altered other changes followed: by far the most significant of these was a growth in urban population, at first slowly but gradually accelerating, especially after the Second World War. The last part of this chapter will place Middle Eastern urban growth and economic development in a broader context, pointing out how much there is in common with other parts of the Third World.

## The nineteenth century and the early twentieth century

During the nineteenth century the economy of many areas in the Middle East was transformed from a largely self-sufficing subsistence economy into a export-oriented economy tied to the industrial economies of Europe and North America. In the absence of mineral reserves — oil was not exploited until the eve of the First World War — the development of agricultural resources was undertaken. The area under cultivation was extended by restoring the law and order essential to irrigation, as in Syria and Iraq, or by building new irrigation works, as in Egypt. Cash crops were introduced and improved. Little serious attempt however was made at industrial development apart from some abortive Egyptian ventures, so native handicrafts suffered badly from the import of European manufactured goods. European capital provided much of the infrastructure for economic development in the form of transport and urban facilities such as gas, water and electricity in the larger cities. Trade and finance were for the most part in the hands of foreign businessmen (Issawi 1966: 9–11).

When European merchants set up business and European factory goods were

[22]

imported in bulk the effect was disastrous for many of the craft guilds in Egypt and the Ottoman Empire. The guilds' conservatism was strong enough to keep the Empire away from the mainstream of European industrial development, and by the time the guilds were officially abolished in 1860 it was too late for such a step to spur industrialization (Herschlag 1964: 21–2). As the industrial structure of the city altered in Egypt, where there were the greatest changes, so too did the administrative structure. The shaikhs of the city quarters were deprived of their fiscal and police functions, which, along with the guilds' regulative functions, became the responsibility of centralized government departments. A new administrative class began to develop and to influence the internal social structure of Egyptian cities. Furthermore, the quarters themselves began to lose their significance as social units. Solidarity among the inhabitants of city quarters was weakened as they became more heterogeneous. There were some exclusively Muslim quarters, but people belonging to different religious communities began to mix and live together in the same district. The feuds between gangs from different quarters appear to have diminished in intensity during the nineteenth century. The religious community in urban Egypt, however, kept its vitality as a social unit even though, like the guilds and the quarters, it ceased to be a body for administration, incidentally depriving the religious functionaries of minority religious communities of their external functions. The Muslim ulama also fared badly. They were deprived of their tax-farming revenues and rapidly lost their former influence and importance, retaining it only in the moral sphere (Baer 1969: 216–20).

The growth of a domestic market in the Middle East had a significant effect on urban–rural relations. A discussion of changes in the nature of urban–rural relations has led I.H. Harik (1972) to question whether urban society did dominate rural society through the type of rent capitalism described by English (1966) in Kirman before the nineteenth century. Prior to the nineteenth century the system of subsistence economy in the Middle East was based on a land tenure system where agricultural land was owned by the state while cultivators and rural notables had the right of usufruct, that is the right of enjoying the use of a property without destroying or wasting its substance. In the non-competitive rural economy land was held by village communities, not the individual; the village shaikh administered the land and treated with the tax farmers. In the Ottoman and Persian Empires tax farmers might cultivate rural estates but had no permanent rights. The revenues accrued directly to the state and could not, in theory, be bequeathed to the tax farmers' descendents. Crops were cultivated for local consumption, and urban as well as rural communities were practically self-sufficient. Villages might sell any surplus to the city, but for the most part grain was removed from the rural areas as tax rather than in trade; that is by force, not exchange. Fruits and vegetables which could not be transported far were grown in or near the city. More than half the population of Cairo was still involved in agriculture in the middle of the nineteenth century (Abu-Lughod 1969: 164) and as recently as 1956 agriculturalists still formed 13 per cent of Kirman's labour force (English 1966: 71).

The nomadic, village and urban sectors of Middle Eastern society all became affected by trade with Europe in this period. Foreign merchants ventured into rural areas to buy agricultural produce for cash, by-passing the wholesale merchants of the ports and the city bazaars. The rapid growth of the domestic market led to some revival of provincial towns by adding to their former administrative or garrison functions, and also to the emergence of new towns and a growth in the size and importance of many ports. Initially, the largest cities lost population due mostly to the decline of native manufactures. The competitive element introduced into the rural scene by giving land a cash value contributed to the introduction of private property in agricultural land (Harik 1972: 349). The state's policy was to give its backing to tribal shaikhs eager to make communally used land their own. Tribal and village communities began to lose their functions as communal bodies, as social differentiation between landed and landless developed (Baer 1969: 62–78). The break-up of traditional community life was thus a feature both of settled rural and urban society during this period. The first phase of modernization in the Middle East, then, saw the growth of a domestic market bound to foreign exports and so to changes in international commodity markets. Money for the first time became the universal medium of exchange. A class of business entrepreneurs entered the rural economy as competitors and collaborators with the state. Provincial towns began to serve as a wholesale market for the hinterland and as administrative centres for the central government, which now had the costly benefits of a modern standing army and a centralized bureaucracy.

The upshot of these trends was a marked change in the location pattern, the size, and the internal structure of cities in the Middle East. Compared with the urban location pattern of previous centuries, there was a shift in orientation towards coastal areas in response to the demand for exports and the opportunities provided by rapid improvements in international communications. The steamship and railway lines, all under European ownership, furthered the integration of the towns they served with the international economy. Seaports of the Mediterranean coast grew steadily in the second half of the nineteenth century, while the Suez canal and increasing British interest in the Gulf encouraged the growth of Jiddah, Aden, Bahrein and Khorramshahr. The expansion of ports' populations was due in some measure to the immigration of many thousands of people such as the Indians, Indonesians and Somalis who moved to the Arabian seaports. In 1907 more than a quarter of the populations of Alexandria and Port Said were foreigners (Issawi 1969: 108–9).

The overall rate of urban growth was slow, however. The rise of the seaports was partly at the expense of smaller towns, and traditional handicrafts were fading out without a concomitant increase in modern industrialization (Issawi 1969: 109–11). The twenty-nine largest towns of Egypt had 400 000 inhabitants in 1821 and 1 596 000 in 1907, but their share of the total population rose only from 9.5 per cent to 14.3 per cent. Syria, already highly physically urbanized long before the nineteenth century, had about 20 to 25 per cent of its total population in towns of

over 10 000 inhabitants, while the proportion of Iraq's population in towns appears
to have been virtually unchanged between 1867 and 1932, at 24 to 25 per cent
(Hasan 1958: 339–50). Estimates for Iran put the urban population at about 15 per
cent of the total of ten million, both figures remaining the same throughout the
century. The 1927 Turkish census recorded 18.5 per cent living in towns over
10 000 inhabitants, from a total of 13 648 000 (Issawi 1969: 108).

A remodelling of the internal social structure and the physical form of some
cities was already under way by the late nineteenth century. In some cities a small,
select suburb began to grow outside the walls of the old Islamic city, so beginning
changes from the pre-industrial city, clearly defined on the ground by its walls, to
the modern settlement with diffuse boundaries that fade off into the surrounding
countryside. Since the Western impact was most immediate on the coastlands of the
Middle East it was the coastal cities, more readily accessible to penetration from the
outside, that tended to change before those of the interior. The general model of an
old city with some new suburbs and the beginnings of new urban functions can be
seen in most instances, though the following three studies of cities on or near the
coast will illustrate that there was a variety of conformations within the model,
depending on the character of the city and country concerned, differences in the
particular specialized functions newly required of the city, dissimilarities between
the styles of the various European countries concerned, and the timing of the
change.

*Abadan: an industrial company town*

Abadan lies on Abadan Island on the left bank of the Shatt al Arab (Karun River) at
the head of the Persian Gulf. The modern city was established by the Anglo Persian
Oil Company, later called the Anglo Iranian Oil Company, following the D'Arcy
concession of 1901, when rights were secured to extract, transport and refine oil
over a vast area of Iran. After oil production began in 1908 pipelines were laid from
the interior to Abadan where one of the largest oil refineries and oil ports in the
world was constructed. A number of European technicians and administrators and a
large number of workers, particularly Bakhtiari tribesmen from the surrounding areas
settled in Abadan. The oil company commissioned the firm of Costain to plan and
lay out a great part of the residential quarters, the refineries and the port. The
population was recorded in 1937 as 60 000 Persian subjects and 950 Europeans
(Admiralty 1945: 496–500).

As an institution the company town is essentially a pioneering device, especially
suited to nations undergoing rapid economic development. Company towns like
Abadan, based on extractive industry, tend to be used as a means of economic
pioneering to open up previously unexplored territory, whereas those based on
manufacturing industry are usually a means of social pioneering, for uplifting and
moulding the worker through the socio-religious ideals of the industrial philanthro-
pist (Porteous 1970). The purpose of Abadan was to refine and export oil, not to

uplift the worker. The Admiralty Handbook of 1942 describes the manner in which
the residential districts were divided so as to separate the higher grade workers,
almost all of them European, from the lower. The residential quarters built by
Costain flanked the refinery on east and west. To the east there was the original
Iranian settlement, Abadan village, nearest the waterfront. It was irregular and
crowded, but northeast from it was Ahmadabad, a new district laid out with a
rectangular road plan, with houses built around traditional courtyards. Many of the
workers, including some immigrants from India, were housed here. The general
impression of Ahmadabad today is one of barrack-like uniformity.

To the west of the refinery were the houses of European staff, with local shops,
cinemas, clubs, a swimming pool and a cricket ground. The suburb was laid out with
avenues and traffic circles like a contemporary housing estate in suburban England.
Acacias and palms grew in gardens protected from the street by neatly clipped
privet hedges. Although the roofs of the houses were flat and the walls the best part
of a metre thick for insulation, the inside was faithful to contemporary English
style in every detail, including the doors of heavy wood with round brass handles
and heavy porcelain bathroom fittings. And here, next to the world's largest oil
refinery, with 7 °C the absolute minimum January temperature, every house had a
grate for a coal fire. House size was carefully graded according to the status of the
occupants, but all had access to the services of a gardener, a houseboy, a cook, a
chauffeur and others, who lived at the back of the house or in Abadan village. All
this, and a large salary, enabled the European company employee to live in a style
to which he was not accustomed at home, and it partly compensated for the bore-
dom and frustration which many felt living in Abadan.

*Misurata: Italian colonial enterprise*

An instance of the effect of direct military conquest and colonial rule from Europe
is provided by Misurata in Libya. The town is located in the easternmost of a series
of oases in western Libya and was an important centre for the caravan trade across
the Sahara until the second half of the nineteenth century when sea transport provided cheaper and swifter means to move goods between Europe and West Africa.
The inhabitants of Misurata were forced to turn to the development of the local
hinterland for sustenance. At the same time numbers of nomads were becoming
sedentary in Misurata's region and the crop surplus which these new farmers began
to produce was sold in the town, so increasing its influence as a market and service
centre. The town was composed of the usual mixture of Arab courtyard houses,
with a market place and, after the Ottoman Empire designated it as the centre of an
administrative district, some barracks and administrative buildings were constructed
(Blake 1968).

These changes were small compared with those effected after their conquest of
Libya between 1911 and 1922 by the Italians. Misurata was proclaimed a provincial
capital and became the regional service centre for huge estates developed locally for

Italian colonists. G. Blake describes how social, economic and physical facilities were constructed, including a hospital, hotel, schools and a cinema, together with banks and a slaughterhouse. The native Misuratans were employed as labourers or simply ignored since they figured little in Mussolini's plans. A small European quarter appeared with its own church, and, as at Abadan, there were efforts to landscape the new town, here in the Italian style, with tiled pavements, a public garden, and roads lined with pink, white and yellow flowering oleanders. There were few efforts to improve the old town. By the end of the Italian occupation in the Second World War the population was about 10 000 souls. In sum, the Italian imprint on Misurata was more in the development of the region's agriculture than in the town; during the occupation numbers of native Misuratans left for Benghazi, Tripoli or abroad, to return en masse when the post-oil boom began in the 1960s (Blake 1975).

## *Tripoli: indigenous growth*

The development of Tripoli in Lebanon during the late nineteenth century contrasts with that of Abadan in that the commercial enterprise was local in origin. The city has a history of international commerce. It served as a Mediterranean port of Aleppo in early Ottoman times but in 1612 the Pasha, the Ottoman Governor, of Tripoli buried alive the French merchants living in the town in an effort to extort money. This immoderate action discouraged European trade for some time. Though there were more French and other mercantile residents in the city in the seventeenth and eighteenth centuries, Tripoli shared in the general urban decline of the Levant at that time. The Western cultural impact on Tripoli began in earnest towards the middle of the nineteenth century. The city had had native Jewish and Christian residents for centuries, but from the middle of the nineteenth century the Christians became the beneficiaries of a number of westernized educational enterprises; schools and colleges, both Roman Catholic and American Protestant were built (Gulick 1967: 29).

At that time Tripoli's population was largely Sunni Muslim, but there were native Jews and Christians living in their own quarters. Most of the Christians were Eastern Orthodox. The aristocratic families among the Christians were primarily merchants, with close connections with the trading communities in Antioch, Latakia and Alexandria. The Muslim aristocratic families derived their wealth primarily from estates in the hinterland and from orchards in the city (Gulick 1967: 27–30).

Tripoli's population expanded between the 1830s and 1914 from about 15 000 to 50 000 (Issawi 1966: 210), despite the massive emigration from the Lebanon which took place in the same period and Tripoli's demotion in the Ottoman administrative structure. Population growth was stimulated by the production of cash crops in the city's hinterland for export, in particular silk, olive oil, tobacco, grain and citrus fruits. The change to a market economy locally and to a renewed role as a port for inland Syria was made possible by improvements in communications: there was a connection in 1895 by a French railway company to Damascus; in 1909 a new carriage road linked Tripoli with Beirut; and in 1911 the French railway company D.H.P. connected Tripoli with Homs and Aleppo. The port was entered and cleared in 1910 by 2 605 vessels (Gulick 1967: 27).

The effects of early commercial expansion on Tripoli's social and physical structure were manifold. After 1881, when a horse tramway was built connecting the old town with the port three kilometres away, several wealthy families built fine new houses among the orchards along the route, disregarding the warnings of those who said that to live outside the city walls was to expose oneself to cutthroats and brigands. More roads were soon built inland from the port, and around the area where these roads met the old city a number of public buildings, modern hotels and mansions were constructed. The city also expanded outside its walls, inland in the direction of the road to Syria, where a less fashionable suburb grew up around the wholesale vegetable distribution centre. Among the facts recorded in 1912 by Baedecker (and it is significant that the Lebanon like Egypt was coming into the international tourist trade), was the presence of fourteen mosques and fourteen churches. Since the Christians made up only one-fifth of the population, the great number of churches is accounted for by the numerous sects and religious orders among them. The foreign schools founded earlier, in the nineteenth century, kept up with the fashion by moving to more spacious premises in the suburbs. The advantages in education these schools gave the Christian community allowed it to derive probably the greatest benefit from the city's commercial growth. By the First World War, however, the bulk of Tripoli's population still lived in the old city, and travellers usuallly remarked on the city's medieval appearance and its lack of electricity or clean water.

## Modern urban development

The First World War saw the collapse of the Ottoman Empire and the beginning of a period of political disunity in the Middle East which has lasted to the present day. The empire would have been broken up completely and all the pieces given to the victorious Western powers if Turkey had not refused to be partitioned and, recovered from humiliation, entered on a period of vigorous internal reform under the leadership of Kemal Ataturk, eschewing any role in the affairs and feuds of the Arab Middle East. Persia, now called Iran, Egypt, Saudi Arabia and the Yemen were independent states, but the British received League of Nations mandates to administer the former Ottoman territories of Palestine, Transjordan and Iraq, while the French received a mandate for Syria. The eventual aim of the mandates, complete independence, was achieved in Iraq in 1932, in Syria in 1945; and in 1948, amidst profound acrimony, Palestine was divided into the states of Israel and Jordan. Territorial nationalism sprang fully armed from the birth of all these new states, as did the ideals of social reform according to the European example, and of national economic enterprises based on the technical, organizational and financial experience of the West.

*Factors in urban growth*

From the 1920s onwards the proportion of people living in urban areas in the
Middle East has risen rapidly, accelerating even further after the Second World War.
The main factors responsible for this growth may conveniently be grouped under
the four headings of political centralization, internal political strife, changes in
foreign trade patterns and foreign relations, and the discovery and exploitation of
oil. Taking the first of these, political centralization: a number of features of
European continental, particularly French, administration including a hierarchy of
areas and of appointed agents had been transplanted to the Ottoman Empire in the
previous century, and a similar German administrative system to Iran (Wickwar
1958). These systems were inherited by the successor states. Their main feature was
centralization of administrative functions. The new states required a network of
regional urban administrative centres to carry through their new policies. Urban
areas grew as a consequence of their new functions, and some were even designated
urban because of these functions rather than their size or economic role. The principal effect of political autonomy in countries such as Iraq, Syria and Lebanon,
however, was further to concentrate political and administrative functions in the
capital.

The political and economic pressures on governments are most direct from urban
populations and at times in the past there has been a tendency to emphasize urban
at the expense of rural development. Between the two world wars further develop-
ments in communications increased the security of both town and countryside, but
new methods of land registration, the extension of irrigation networks and the
gradual displacement of the camel by mechanized transport limited the scope of
nomadic tribespeople. The transfer of land from tribal to shaikh ownership in Iraq
worsened the lot of the peasant as it had done in Egypt in the previous century.
Already, before the Second World War, the increase in the urban labour reserve
which resulted from rural to urban migration and the lack of industrial growth was
causing concern to politicians and economists, and it had an increasing influence on
the shaping of political consciousness, as is shown by the changes in political slogans
(Herschlag 1964: 163).

Internal political strife, too, has played a part in encouraging urban growth
through unsettling large numbers of people. In the years after 1914, for example,
about 50 000 Armenians moved into Aleppo as refugees from wholesale massacres
being conducted by Kurds (at the instigation of the Turks). The establishment of
Israel resulted in the moving of 900 000 Palestinians, many of whom took up residence in such cities as Amman, Kuwait, Beirut and Riyadh. Instability within
countries, following coups and changes of regime, has prompted sizeable numbers
to move to cities (Ffrench & Hill 1971: 5–6).

The Suez canal, opened in 1869, and more recently the growth of international
air traffic have once more emphasized the Middle East's geographical position at the
crossroads between Asia, Europe and Africa. Ports, cities with international airports,

and places of tourism or pilgrimage have directly benefited from the reorientation. Other changes in foreign relations and trade have also influenced urban growth and development. The principal agents of economic change in Egypt, the Levant and Turkey in the nineteenth and early twentieth centuries were foreigners. They performed many of the 'middle class' activities in commerce and administration. When foreigners, such as the Italians in Libya, and other minority groups were expelled they made way for indigenes to take over their functions, thus providing opportunities for local enterprise. More recently the supply of foreign aid from a wide variety of sources has further focussed attention on the cities as points of external contact with the aid-giving countries. Whether the aid is civil or military the ultimate beneficiaries are usually the urban population.

Lastly, oil has contributed to urban growth and development by creating direct and indirect employment and by making capital available for investment. Direct employment has been provided in oil camps, at tanker terminals and in the refining industry, at places like Abadan, Bahrein, Kirkuk and Haifa. In the early phases of oil production most of the oil was refined in the Middle East; but changes in the structure of demand, improvements in tanker technology, and political and strategic considerations have made the oil-importing countries try to do as much refining as possible near the market. The trend has more recently been reversed as the increased power of the producers has allowed them to insist on more refining in the producer countries.

Indirect employment opportunities are greatest in the capital cities where the services needed by the nationalized oil companies provide numerous openings for economic enterprise. The oil revenues accruing to the states of the Middle East either indirectly, as in Lebanon and Egypt, or directly have had a major influence on the physical expansion of the urban areas and on the growth of their populations. But the distribution of monies is by no means even. Kuwait, one of the world's largest oil producers, had a population of about 800 000 in 1970, comparable to Liverpool, England, or Cleveland, Ohio. Iran's oil revenues are spent for the benefit of 32 million inhabitants, while Turkey with a population of over 37 million has practically no oil-export revenues at all.

*Urban population growth*

It must be emphasized then that the growth of cities in the Middle East is taking place within a series of widely differing circumstances though the arbitrary nature of many of the boundaries between countries has not prevented them from developing each towards a progressively greater demographic individuality (Clarke 1972: 18). Details of the rate of urban growth for each country are given below (in descending order of size), though because data are available in slightly different forms and over different periods for each country strict comparability is not always possible.

*Turkey*: Between 1935 and 1950 the urban population as a proportion of the total rose only from 17.6 per cent to 18.7 per cent, involving a numerical increase of 1.3 million, or 47.1 per cent, compared with a total population growth of just under 30 per cent. From 1950 to 1965, however, the urban element increased by 138 per cent, a numerical growth of 5.4 million people to 9.3 million, 29.8 per cent of the total population; and in the five years 1960—5 urban areas increased in population by 23.5 per cent, 2.2 million, compared with 7.4 per cent in rural areas. Fertility is much lower in the large towns than the small and is lower in the small towns than the rural areas. Migration clearly plays an important part in urban growth (Dewdney 1972: 54).

*Egypt*: Urban population in Egypt was put at 1.4 million persons in 1899, 14.5 per cent of the total of 9.7 million. Between 1937 and 1960 there was a rapid rise in population and especially in the urban population, rising to 12.4 million people, or 41 per cent of the total of 30 million in 1966 (Mountjoy 1972: 301).

*Iran*: The urban population of Iran rose from 2.1 million to 3.2 million between 1900 and the 1940s, though it remained at 21 per cent of the total population. The urban proportion increased to 31 per cent of the total in 1956 and in 1966 to 39 per cent. The largest cities of 100 000 or more increased their percentage of the total urban population from 51.3 to 60.6 in the same period. The total urban population in 1966 was 10.6 million, compared with a rural total of 16.5 million people. The urban annual growth rate was 2.9 per cent and the rural 1.7 per cent; and since fertility is lower in the large urban areas, this suggests that migration is accounting for differences in growth rates between the cities and the countryside (Bharier 1968; Clark 1972: 84—90).

*Iraq*: The level of Iraq's urban population remained constant between 1867 and 1930 at about 25 per cent of the total though the numbers living in cities rose from 310 000 to 808 000 people. The annual growth rate for cities between 1957 and 1965 was 5.7 per cent, compared with a national rate of 3.5 per cent. Fertility is thought to be higher in the urban areas than the rural areas and by 1965, with the additional boost of migration, the urban population was 3.6 million, forming 43.9 per cent of the 8.2 million total (Lawless 1972).

*Syria*: From 1940 to 1960 Syria's total population rose from 2.5 million to 4.3 million, and to 5.3 million in 1965, and further by 1970 to 6.9 million. The evidence suggests that urban growth has been rapid, rising from 37 per cent of the total population in 1960 to perhaps over 40 per cent by 1970. Damascus and Aleppo were of comparable size in 1970, being 835 000 and 639 000 respectively (Dewdney 1972: 130—42).

*Saudi Arabia*: Estimates have put the increase in Saudi Arabia's urban population between 1932 and 1962—3 at about 170 per cent, from about 300 000 to 800 000 persons, and increasing to 1.3 million in 1969–70. The urban population between 1962–3 and 1969–70 is estimated to have increased from 24 per cent of the total of 3.3 million to 33 per cent of a total of 4 million, absorbing half of the settled population's increase and all of the nomadic population's increase through migration (McGregor 1972: 236–7).

*Lebanon*: The absence of reliable census data for Lebanon makes comparison of urban size over time difficult. It is thought that by 1970 Beirut's population was 700 000, or one million for 'Greater Beirut', making perhaps 40 per cent of the country's total (Fisher 1972: 150). It was suggested by Yaukey (1961) that in the long term there are only slight variations in fertility rates between rural and urban areas.

*Israel*: As defined by the armistice lines of 1948, Israel had a total population of 873 000 of which 73.6 per cent was living in towns. However, by 1967 this had risen to 81.6 per cent of a total of 2.7 million. Immigration accounted for much of the rise in total population (Blake 1972: 191–4).

*Jordan*: The set of census figures available for Jordan, dating from 1961 give as urban 43.9 per cent of the total of 1.7 million (Fisher 1972: 212–13).

*Libya*: There were occasional spurts of urban growth in Libya during the first sixty years of the present century, but after 1960 when oil revenues began to flow there was a sudden rise in the rate of growth. The proportion of the total population which was living in settlements with more than 20 000 persons rose from 18 per cent to 25 per cent between 1954 and 1966. The total population in 1966 was 1.84 million (Hartley 1972: 325–8).

*Kuwait*: The urban population was 94 per cent of the 1965 total of 467 000; and this exceptionally high proportion is unlikely to have diminished in the period up to 1970 when the state's population increased to about 800 000, of which nearly half are non-citizens who have immigrated since 1945 or who have been born in the immigrant community (Hill 1972: 242–73).

*The Gulf States*: The other micro-states of the Persian Gulf are beginning to show the same pattern of urban population concentration as Kuwait. In each case the capital dominates the urban scene. Until recently, however, immigration has been controlled, and the possibilities for rural to urban migration confined to those who live within the boundaries of the states (Hill 1972: 242–73).

Summarizing for the Middle East as a whole, a number of points emerge. First, urban growth has been fastest since 1930. Ports and capital cities have shown tremendous increases. Amman in 1966 was over ten times larger than in the 1930s;

Tehran added 1.2 million inhabitants in ten years between 1956 and 1966; Cairo and Alexandria both doubled in size in the years between 1947 and 1966 and now account for one-fifth of Egypt's total. Second, most of the countries now have more than one-third of the population living in towns, making the Middle East more physically urbanized than most of Tropical Africa, or of East, Southeast and South Asia.

The countries of the Middle East have been discussed above in descending order of size to stress the third point, that the proportion of population living in cities tends to be inversely related to the size of the state and directly related to the size of the modern sector. J.I. Clarke has pointed out that traditions of urbanism appear to have little relationship to present levels of urban population (1972: 28); thus, Jordan has a larger proportion of town dwellers than Syria. The final point worth noting here is that despite the relatively low proportions of urban population in the largest countries, they do have most of the large cities and most of the town dwellers. In the most recent censuses the number of localities with 100 000 inhabitants or more in Egypt, Turkey and Iran totalled forty-five, whereas there was a total of eighteen in all the other countries together.

## Migration and urban growth

How far urban growth in the Middle East has been due to migration and how far to differential natural growth rates between rural and urban areas is a matter in some doubt, if only because there is no uniform pattern throughout the region. Urban and rural fertility patterns in Egypt, for instance, are much the same; but urban mortality is substantially below rural areas, so the cities have a greater excess of births over deaths than rural areas (Abu-Lughod 1963). In several countries differential fertility and mortality as well as selective migration create concentrations of the very young and the very old in rural areas and concentrations of the most active age groups in the larger cities.

It is implicit in the discussion so far that migration and natural growth are independent of one another. That, of course, is not so. The sequence of events for many major cities appears to involve firstly rapid growth resulting from migration and then within less than a generation a much higher rate of natural increase in the city than in the rural areas because of the youth of the immigrant population and lower death rates. Migration in absolute terms is important in Baghdad, Tehran, Cairo, and other major cities, but it is also an important primer for future urban natural increase.

Kuwait provides a useful illustration of this process, for here the distinction between native and immigrant populations is maintained by differences in citizenship. It is possible to isolate the immigrant population in the census and compare it with the Kuwaiti citizen population. Kuwait is also probably the most spectacular example of the Alladin's Lamp of the oil industry being able apparently to summon a major city out of the desert, where very little existed before. A tiny, insignificant shaikhdom in the nineteenth century, Kuwait relied on pearl fishing, ship building, local handicrafts and an entrepot trade centred on the port of Kuwait City. It came under British influence and protection towards the end of the century, and in 1907 it had an estimated population of 35 000, nearly all in Kuwait City. Natural increase of population was negligible in Kuwait even until 1950, and all demographic growth may be attributed to migration. Kuwait never possessed a rural agricultural population, the interior of the state being desert, and the great bulk of the migrants were from outside the country. Total population grew from an estimated 60 000 in the 1930s to 100 000 at the end of the Second World War, 160 000 by 1952, 467 339 in 1965, and is estimated to rise by 1976 to between 900 000 and one million people.

Prior to the discovery of oil Kuwait's population consisted of a cosmopolitan blend of people from the Gulf littorals, from South Asia, and a slave-descended Negroid strain from East Africa, mixed together in the city (Ffrench & Hill 1971: 21). There was no distinction between Kuwaiti and non-Kuwaiti until in 1948 when a citizenship law was approved. The stimulus for the distinction was oil. Kuwait began exporting oil in 1946, when the Kuwait Oil Company's labour force was 1 552. This grew to 8 753 in 1948. The expansion of Kuwait City and its service facilities gained momentum in the 1950s, and as personal prosperity rose through the disbursal of public money to Kuwaiti citizens immigration on an enormous scale began. Non-Kuwaitis, that is immigrants and their descendants, constituted in 1957 some 45 per cent of the population, rising by 1965 to 53 per cent. The source of the migrants has gradually changed from the earlier decades when most were from the Gulf states, Iran, Oman and elsewhere, to later years when they have been reduced in proportion though not in numbers, while Arabs from further afield, Jordanians, Syrians, Lebanese and Egyptians have increased.

This distinction between immigrant groups by place of origin can be extended further to the type of employment a migrant can expect on arrival, and to the demographic structures of these groups. Among the changes in demographic structure identified by Hill (1972) between 1957 and 1965 was an increase from 274 to 423 non-Kuwaiti females per thousand non-Kuwaiti males. The more even balance in migrants' sex ratios shows that more whole families were immigrating. It might be added that the high birth rates of non-Kuwaitis will tend to balance total sex ratios since, naturally, approximately equal numbers of girls and boys will be born. Literacy rates among migrants also rose, pointing to a greater sophistication in the influx of foreigners. A contrast still exists between Iranians, Syrians, Omanis and other people from the Gulf states, whose populations have a strong male bias of over 70 per cent in Kuwait, and Jordanians, Saudis, Lebanese and Iraqis with a bias between 61 and 64 per cent. The latter groups had a better job expectancy than the others, since they had higher levels of literacy and technical training. Consequently, the better salaries they can command means they can better afford to bring dependants to Kuwait.

The extent to which Kuwait's rapid growth rates may be attributed to natural increase as well as migration may be seen by looking at birth, death and fertility rates. Kuwait's health service has few parallels in the Middle East and compares favourably with many European health services. A population with high birth and death rates before 1946 gained access to modern medical services, free to both Kuwaitis and non-Kuwaitis, within a few years. Death rates quickly fell, in particular infant death rates, with the result that Kuwait now has a broad-based age–sex pyramid, with one of the youngest populations in the world. Crude birth rates, the number of births per thousand of the total population, for non-Kuwaitis are well below those for Kuwaitis, principally because so many non-Kuwaitis are unmarried males, or married with their families abroad. Death rates, however, are also lower among non-Kuwaitis, since so many of them are young persons in the economically active age groups and less at risk than the very young or the old. On the other hand the rate of natural increase, the difference between crude birth rates and crude death rates, is higher among Kuwaitis; but the fertility rate, that is the proportion of live births per thousand women aged 15–44 years is higher among non-Kuwaitis (Hill 1972: 244–55).

Thus, to determine the relative weight to be given to immigration or natural increase is no easy task, depending as it does on the precise definition of 'immigrant' that is used, and whether one includes second generation migrants in that category. Kuwait would seem to confirm that native natural increase is important to the increase in urban population, but so too are the results of immigration, both in the movement of persons into the city and in the birth of their children there.

## City size and economic development

Concentration of the urban population in one or two of the largest cities in each of the Middle Eastern countries, suggesting as it does an over-concentration of numbers and urban amenities, has given rise to some discussion. Turkey, Iran and Saudi Arabia are the only countries with less than 20 per cent of their total population, rural or urban, in their two largest cities. Regularities in the relation between the size of cities and their rank in a region or country have been observed and formalised in numerous instances in developed countries. According to G.K. Zipf (Berry 1973) this relationship should ideally be such that, when the cities are ranked in descending order of size and plotted in a graph prepared on double-logarithmic paper with population on one axis and rank on the other, the plot forms a straight line. Or, put another way, the population of the second largest city should be half that of the largest city, the population of the tenth largest city should be one-tenth that of the largest city, and so on. Enough evidence is now available, according to Haggett (1972: 284), to prove that regular rank-size chains are recognizable for settlements in many different regions and many different time periods.

Turkey and Jordan have the only city-size distributions in the Middle East which conform to this rank–size relationship. However, below the city ranked fifth in size in each country, and except for Bahrein, the curves for all the countries regardless

2. Rank–size relationships for cities of the Middle East

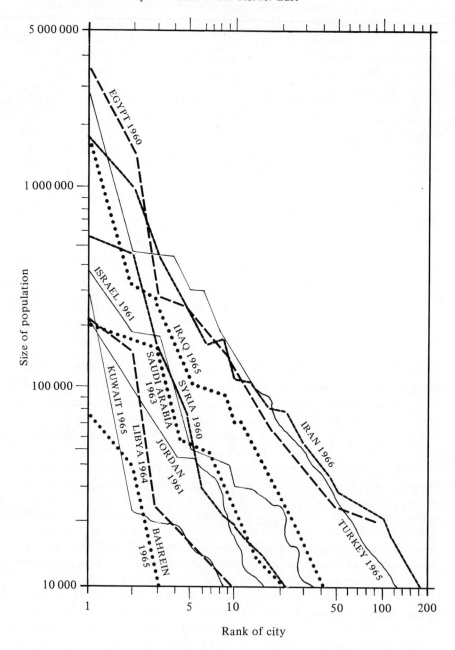

of size, are remarkably similar in conforming to the relationship. Above the fifth-ranked city Iran, Iraq and Kuwait have one overwhelmingly predominant city, a condition known as primacy, while Egypt and Syria have two predominant cities, a condition sometimes known as dual primacy.

What is the significance of these distributions with regard to economic development and social change? The principal result of primacy among the cities of the developing world in general has been regarded as 'parasitism' (Breese 1969), where the largest city consumes a disporportionate amount of the country's wealth. Hoselitz (1955) has divided cities into two categories of 'generative' and 'parasitic'; cities in the former category are said to stimulate the growth of the wider region in which they are located, while 'parasitic' cities act as a curb rather than a stimulus to growth. A key factor in the behaviour of the parasitic city is the dissipation of wealth derived from the surrounding region in non-productive urban consumption.

This notion of 'parasitic' cities has been linked to that of 'overurbanization', implying that many non-Western countries in the early stages of industrial development have a higher percentage of people living in town than their present stage of economic development can adequately maintain. Overurbanization (in the physical sense) is said to be the end result of excessive rural to urban migration of the unemployed or the inadequately employed in advance of adequate expansion of urban employment opportunities; and the juxtaposition of a small advanced urban economic centre and the large traditional economic centre which employs the migrants and those left in the villages is claimed to result in a condition known as a dual economy. The concepts of parasitism, physical overurbanization and dualistic economies have been linked by a number of social scientists and it has been held that they are productive of alienation, *anomie* and social disorganization (Berry 1973: 98–9).

The concept of overurbanization has been applied to Egypt by Abu-Lughod (1965*a*), who found that overurbanization was less in evidence, with only about 35 per cent of the total population then living in cities than overconcentration in the two largest cities, Cairo and Alexandria. The Egyptian case does provide evidence of dissipation of national resources in non-productive consumption, for the money spent on modernizing Cairo and Alexandria in the nineteenth century helped lead eventually to the bankruptcy of the state and occupation by foreign powers (Abu-Lughod 1965*b*: 429–57). That, however, was long before the modern flood of migrants to the city in this century. The reasons cited by Abu-Lughod (1965*a*: 318ff) why overconcentration may not be desirable are both social and economic: the plight of these large cities in absorbing large numbers of migrants during their transition from a rural to an urban way of life may be added to the rising economic costs per head of providing municipal and private services once population exceeds an optimum point of several hundred thousand; it is argued that the very size and unfamiliarity of metropolitan centres inhibits the attempts of smaller communities to emulate them; and the concentration of the urban site in one place may impede the goal of improving rural life.

Similar points for the Middle East in general are made by Issawi (1969: 117—19), who records that Tehran in 1965 consumed 40 per cent of Iran's electricity and 50 per cent of oil products, that Baghdad in 1953 accounted for 65 per cent of Iraq's physicians and Istanbul in 1950 had 25 per cent of Turkey's physicians. The main explanation advanced by Issawi is administrative centralization, with the growth of economic planning and an attendant growth in bureaucracy. Among the disadvantages of this concentration are that it encourages people of talent to move to the metropolitan centres, where the rewards are greatest, while at the same time the spread of modern culture to the rest of the country is limited.

Yet before the city-size distributions of the Middle East, with their tendency to show concentrations of urban population in one or two cities, are regarded as malignant deviations from the rank—size rule, and before the Middle East's primate cities are labelled 'parasites', we should perhaps decide whether such a distribution can be expected to apply in the context of the Middle East. Following a study of the urban growth process in 38 countries with examples from all parts of the world Berry (1961) has concluded that primate rank—size patterns are a product of urban growth in countries which are smaller than average; have a short history of physical urbanization; and are economically or politically simple. Conversely log-normal distributions are the product of city development in countries which are larger than average; with a long history of physical urbanization; and which are economically or politically complex. Hypotheses that the proportion of a country's population living in cities or the degree of economic development account for size distributions are unsupported by empirical evidence. In the light of this analysis the rank—size distributions of the Middle East still show no simple pattern: Israel and Saudi Arabia fall into none of the three categories which might explain their log-normal distributions, while Iran's primacy cannot be accounted for by its size, history of urbanization, or political make-up.

An explanation why most Middle Eastern countries do not conform to expectations about city-size distributions may be found in the different labour market conditions which obtain there compared to those in the developed world. A comparison of labour market conditions in the developed world with those in the Third World in general has been made by Berry (1973: 91—9). Industrial urban growth in the United States and Western Europe took place initially in economic core regions, and when sustained over a long period economic growth produced high labour-shortages and high wage-rates. Labour intensive industries shifted to smaller urban centres or more peripheral areas, thus stimulating growth further away from the core. At the same time regions within the continental United States, or within the European colonial empires, tended to specialize according to their resource endowments. Cities and their secondary support industries became the means whereby the specialized sub-regions were reticulated into national and imperial economies. The balanced system of cities which resulted, with each city performing its function and within its field of influence successively smaller settlements each performing their regional functions, would have a 'normal' rank—size distribution. In such a system settlements are also spaced with regularity according to size, the larger being further apart and the smaller settlements more closely spaced. It has been suggested that such a system, with its straight-line size relationships, reflected the achievement of national unity in political and in economic terms.

In the primate systems of the Middle East, by contrast, there has been little filtering down of industry from the capital to the regions because wages in the major cities are maintained at a low level by a greater influx of migrants to the cities than occurred in the developed world. There has been no incentive to decentralize, and modern enterprise has remained in the metropolitan centres, despite government efforts to plan national economies and regional growth. According to Berry, however, increasing primacy may be almost beneficial, in that it is a sign that economic growth is taking place, albeit in one place, and is affecting more people. On the other hand generalizing costs per person for activities such as education, public or private transport and provision of power suggests that middle-sized cities of around 100 000 may be more efficient than either very large metropolises or small towns. Above one million population these activities become progressively more expensive (Morrill 1970: 157).

Some further points specific to the Middle East can be made. The urban systems of the area have been discussed within the framework of national boundaries which in many cases are only a few decades old and were arbitrarily drawn in the first place. The cities of Iraq or of Syria for example are being moulded by the economic demands and the transport systems of the modern state, within national boundaries fixed only since the end of the First World War. In countries where provincialism is strong it may be more appropriate to look at regional city systems as well as the national system. The urban pattern in Iran before the present century was one of regional groups of cities around the agriculturally sterile desert that occupies the centre of the country. In contrast to Egypt, the complete dominance of Iran's capital dates only from the present century. At the provincial level capitals like Isfahan and Shiraz are strongly primate with regard to local rank—size distributions, and at even lower regional levels cities like Qom, Yazd or Kirman are many times larger than the largest settlement in their region (Clark & Costello 1973). The reason for these and similar patterns in the Middle East may be the gaps which exist in the hinterlands of cities at all size levels. The semi-arid geographical environment has made rural life precarious outside the irrigated, intensively cultivated nuclei and there are spatial discontinuities in the settled area (Issawi 1969: 118). Clustering of settlements about a resource is a common feature in settlement geography, to be found on coalfields or around a water supply; and in each case it affects the size and distance relationships between settlements.

Our analysis so far shows that physical urbanization in the Middle East has much in common with the experience of other parts of the Third World. That contemporary urban growth has resulted largely from the expansion of capitalist enterprise is perhaps the factor above all which distinguishes it from pre-industrial urban development. Social urbanization in the Middle East is a phenomenon of urban population growth resulting from migration and natural increase together; some of this growth has occurred around pre-industrial urban centres and some on new sites, so that the present size of urban populations frequently bears little spatial relation to traditions of urban life. Traditional urban life nonetheless in many ways provides a model for the conduct of contemporary urban life, and it accounts for some of the qualities of social urbanization peculiar to the Middle East. Succeeding chapters will show the social consequences of urban population growth, dealing initially with why people move to the towns and what happens to them when they get there.

# 4. Rural – urban migration

We have seen that in statistical terms the numbers of migrants in some cities may not be as important to urban growth as natural increase, though migration of young people who then have their children in the city is an important primer to rapid urban growth. However, the communication links between village and city, the reasons why migrants move, and where they live when they arrive, are an integral part of the process of social change in the city.

## Communication between city and village

Permanent migration to the city is only one of a number of types of movement and communication between the countryside and the city. These vary from country to country and from village to village, and factors which impede communication in one area assist communication in another. Villages vary considerably in social characteristics and in consequence have different communication patterns. One classification by R.A. Fernea (1972: 75–98) suggests nearly a dozen categories of village, based on the villages' degree of tribal organization, urban influence, and their political or economic dominance or independence. Thus, for example, in villages which are tribally organized with a high degree of urban dominance and subject to the political dominance of the city, such as Kallorwan, a Druze village in Lebanon, tribal affiliations and ties may link village and town through national politics. Tribally organized villages with local private ownership of resources and means of production, such as many of those described by F. Barth (1953) in southern Kurdistan, may have a high degree of independence from urban centres. Another type, villages which are under a high degree of urban influence, economically dominated by the city, but lacking tribal organization are found around the traditional cities of the central Iranian plateau.

One such city, similar in many respects to Kirman, Qom, Yazd or Semnan, is Kashan. The administrative district of which Kashan is the centre, the *shahrestan*, covers part of the Kargas mountains and part of the central plateau. The province has been controlled until the recent past by an urban upper class, which owned land and water rights, and carpet contracts, as well as being the only source of credit. Contact between property owners and villages was maintained by agents who travelled from city to village. In the lowlands topography and natural proximity have allowed easy intercommunication, but in the highlands contacts are confined within individual valleys and groups of valleys, where, cut off from one another in the winter by snowfalls on the intervening mountains, the easiest routes of access

[41]

are down valley to the lowlands and the city. The more remote valleys have preserved their economic independence from the city: villagers own the land themselves
and weave carpets on their own account. The shahrestan is governed from the city,
from where local political and administrative appointments are made in the villages
and all disputes other than minor, local ones are referred to the courts there. Each
of the government ministries is represented in the city and from their offices instructions are issued to government officials, such as the Literacy Corps and the Health
Corps, and the instruments of bureaucratic control in the villages.

Travel between the villages and Kashan City is mostly by bus. Many of the larger
villages have a vehicle, owned collectively or by one of the wealthier citizens; the
largest villages and those near Kashan City have more than one. Buses travel to the
city in the morning and return in the evening, but the nearest villages have several
trips a day. While weekday visits are mostly for shopping and business, on Fridays
(the day of obligatory assembly at the mosque for prayer) when the shops are shut,
most visits are social. Numbers of peasants still ride in by donkey and some travel
out by the same means to work in the fields of the city's oasis. City dwellers also
visit the villages, particularly during the summer, when many travel to the mountains to escape the heat of the lowlands. Often they stay with relatives. Frequently
the women and children go, leaving the menfolk behind. The present routeway
pattern in Kashan province, although it has been expanded by the demands of
modern wheeled traffic, is the same in outline as it was in the nineteenth century,
and probably dates back at least as far as the twelfth century, when the boundaries
of the city province corresponded closely with those of the present day. So this
pattern of summer migration which is not uncommon in the Middle East, has been
established for the wealthy for centuries. The dominance of the city, and of one particular city, Kashan, is not new. In 1889 E.G. Browne, when discussing one village
dialect with a villager learnt that the dialect phrases: 'I am going to the city' and 'I
am going to Kashan' were synonymous. This is still the case today (Costello 1976).

Kashan illustrates well the point made by L. Nader (1965) that communication
which stems from national or foreign interest moves predominantly from city to
village, while communication which arises from personal or individual interest is
usually reciprocal between urbanite and villager. In the latter case, for example,
Lebanese villagers come into contact with city dwellers when a conflict between
two village groups is referred by the antagonists to someone living outside the village
who is willing to act as intermediary. This person may arrange a remedy to the problem informally, out of court. The scene for negotiations will be on neutral ground,
away from the village, most often in the private home of the mediator, who may be
a lawyer, a would-be politician, government representative or other, and who acts in
return for perhaps money, prestige, or political support.

## The causes of migration

The initial causes of rural to urban migration may be summarized conveniently under 'pull' and 'push' factors. The balance between them varies, of course, from individual to individual and from region to region. Taking the first of these, many inhabitants of villages and small towns are attracted to the big cities by the better, brighter life they believe awaits them there. J. Abu-Lughod (1961: 23) considers that large numbers of youths, their aspirations fed by education and literacy, migrate to Cairo where they are rapidly assimilated into urban life. A study of the motives of non-dependant migrants in Tehran between 1956 and 1966 indicated that 17 per cent were seeking a better job, and 5.2 per cent were there for education, though many of these came from other cities. But 72 per cent came seeking a job or a better job. The higher wages in Tehran, more than double those of similar labourers in the rest of the country, were a strong incentive. Marriage was the motive for 11 per cent of the 235 000 migrants studied. Arranged marriages where former migrants returned to Tehran with their wives after going to their home village or town to marry were the most common (Bahrambeygui 1972: 49–50). Elsewhere in the Middle East centres of economic growth, particularly those like Kuwait which are associated with the oil industry, have attracted migrants. But the availability of employment does not itself imply that large-scale migration will take place, even in an area with a countryside as poor as much of the rural Middle East. Some states in the Gulf impose restrictions on immigrants, thus reducing the numbers living in urban areas; and in the case, for instance, of Kashan, large-scale immigration from rural areas to Kashan City has not happened, despite the fact that the city has a rapidly expanding modern textile industry, flourishing commerce, and close ties with its rural hinterland. On the face of it, Kashan provides an ideal attraction for rural migrants, but the attractions of Tehran are greater, or the urge to leave the rural areas not strong enough (Costello 1976).

Migrants to Baghdad, especially those from Iraq's southern provinces, also move principally for economic reasons. The monthly income of a migrant to Baghdad, whatever his training, can equal the total of his former annual income from farming in Amara province. Furthermore, a migrant can select the type of work he wants and he is no longer working for a landlord, nor does his income go to moneylenders. Interviews of Amara migrants conducted by M. Azeez (1968) revealed that some migrants had been living by stealing in Amara, but were now successful shopkeepers and grocers in Baghdad. Improvements in nutrition resulted from the migrants' higher income. Fighting might occur over a water melon found floating in a river or marsh in Amara, but there was no difficulty in buying a variety of fruits and veg-etables in the city. Education and health services were mentioned as important attractions in Baghdad, and once in the city migrants became the beneficiaries of government projects to improve housing and to provide water, transport, electricity and other services. The interviewed migrants wrote home to their relatives and friends in the villages describing the agreeable way of life in the city. As a result, many still living in Amara lost their enthusiasm in farming and in participating in rural life. Nevertheless, 20 per cent of the interviewees in Baghdad said they could be persuaded to return to Amara (Azeez 1968: 267–327).

During the present century the Middle East has seldom been free from political turmoil causing widespread movement of people to cities. Palestinians have been widely scattered since the foundation of Israel in 1948. Many of the poorer found their way to the 'bidonvilles' of Beirut, there to form their own communities along-side native Beirutis and people from the poverty-stricken areas in southern Lebanon. Another instance was the forcible transfer of Turkish communities from the Aegean Islands to mainland Turkey following the Treaty of Lausanne in 1923. One group of about 400 persons arrived eventually in the town of Bodrum, where they transformed many aspects of local life and economy, teaching the locals to eat new foods, like ripe tomatoes and seafood, which they had not eaten before either because they did not know of their existence or because of local superstitions about them (Mansur 1972: 10). A further example is the movement of Kurdish tribesmen to the major centres of the Ottoman Empire during the years before the First World War. The subsequent growth of a Kurdish educated class resulted in the growth and revival of Kurdish national consciousness. More recently fighting between Kurdish nationalist forces and Iraqi government forces with the destruction of villages by the Iraqi air force has precipitated the movement of migrants from the countryside to urban centres in the Kurdish districts of Iraq (Lawless 1972: 104). Government policies to pacify and settle nomads have had influence elsewhere. Under Reza Shah (1925–41) some Iranian tribes were compelled to send a proportion of their children to elementary schools. Some stayed and found employment in the cities and some returned educated to their tribe (Clarke and Clark 1969: 22). Conscription to the armed forces has introduced young men throughout the Middle East to mechanical civilization and some modern education, moving them away from home, frequently to spend some time in barracks in the cities. There is also the situation in Israel, where many of the migrants into the country have begun to live in cities for the first time. This is less so for European and North American immigrants than for the Jews from North Africa and the Yemen.

Besides the 'push' factors in migration which are political in origin there are economic pressures to move. The intensity of these pressures varied from country to country and from region to region. Rural to urban migration in Turkey is not recorded as such in the censuses, but there is evidence that it is greater on the coastal fringes of the country than in the interior, and within the interior it is greater in the west than the east. This reflects marked regional differences in level of economic development, for the modernization of agriculture has proceeded much further in the coastal zones and has been more effective in the west than the east. Rural population density is greatest in Trabzon province on the Black Sea coast, where an assortment of crops supports a large population at a level which, for Turkey, may be regarded as one of modest prosperity. However, there are indications here of a certain pressure on resources which is countered by a steady flow of migration westwards (Dewdney 1971: 174; 1972: 48–65). In Libya also the provinces display differing patterns of migration both within the provinces and between them. Three-quarters of the migrants recorded in the 1964 census originated in Tripolitania, which has the country's largest concentration of population. Most travelled to the city of Tripoli, which has a central location in relation to its fertile hinterland. In the coastal region to the east of Tripoli declining water tables have increased pressure on local resources and tens of thousands have moved, helped by easy transport to Tripoli. In the Fezzan, Libya's southern province within the Sahara, difficult drainage, high water tables, over-exploitation of the land and intense evaporation have caused much potentially fertile land in the oases to become saline, and the area under cultivation has decreased by 50 per cent since 1900 (Hartley 1972: 323–32).

These examples from Turkey and Libya show that migration from rural areas tends to be prevalent where there is local pressure of population upon available resources. Rural problems may partly be eased by remittances sent to villages by rural migrants in the city. It is not uncommon for villagers in the Egyptian Delta and in Lebanon to work away from the village while maintaining a season or permanent residence there. Legal and political registration may be retained in the village. As early as the latter part of the nineteenth century Lebanese villagers were investing monies saved in the city in improving the amenities of the villages by paving streets, opening fountains, having roofs tiled, and such like (Antoun & Harik 1972: 8–10).

Government attitudes to the countryside have altered with the coming to power of reformist, populist regimes, resulting in the case of Turkey from the 'ruralising election' of 1952, when the Democratic Party came to power. In Turkey, Egypt, Iran, Iraq and other countries there has been some measure of agricultural reform to attempt to improve the agriculturalists' lot. Land Reform by government edict usually transfers land from former owners to tenants and new owners. The functions which landlords frequently filled of providing capital, credit and an outlet for agricultural surplus are now performed in many areas by marketing and farm management co-operatives and government-subsidized credit arrangements. At the same time agricultural reform has involved the modernization of agriculture in some parts, frequently through the consolidation of formerly fragmented holdings and the introduction of machines, improved and often large-scale irrigation projects, and new crops. The principal aims of these measures from the government's point of view are to raise productivity per hectare and per worker, so producing more crops for the economy and increasing rural incomes. Together with the health, education and welfare services in the villages these measures are partly intended to keep the peasants on the land and out of the cities.

The effect may be the opposite to that intended. Experience of agricultural reform in many parts of the world has shown that per capita incomes in rural areas can only rise in the long term if people leave the land. This may be so in parts of the Middle East. Mechanization requires fewer workers, not more, given the same basic resources, and Land Reform seldom caters for all who work on the land. For instance, under the current Land Reform programme in Iran land was granted only to those families who formerly enjoyed tenancy and cultivation rights. Farm labourers and non-farm labourers were left out, so stimulating bitter class conscious-

ness in some villages (Ajami 1969), and providing further incentive to leave. Governments have also extended the area of farm land through irrigation schemes and the
reclamation of desert and marsh. The most spectacular of such schemes has been the
Aswan High Dam in Egypt. But here the growth of population has overtaken the
government's efforts. The crop area per head fell by more than 25 per cent between
1947 and 1965 (Mountjoy 1972: 310).

Two contrasting areas will serve to exemplify this central problem of the pressure
of population on resources, one in Iran, the other in the Tigris—Euphrates lowlands.
First, H. Bowen-Jones on Iran:

In the high valleys and terraces of the northern Zagros and Alburz ranges, in the
isolated central mountains at Tezerjān and on Kūh-I-Taftān in Balūchistan, as everywhere in the highlands of the Middle East, lushness and fertility seem to dwell,
accentuated by contrast with the low plains. It is important however that the visual
impact made by rows of poplar, the groves of almond and apricot and the steps of
terraced fields, with their variety of pulses, legumes and vegetables should not
deceive the traveller into believing that rustic plenty abounds. Even the intensity of
production which exists has been developed only by strenuous uncosted manual
labour which has to be expended more and more prodigally as growing populations
impose increasing strains on the inexorably restricted resources of topographically
usable land. Here lies the paradox of apparent plenty and real poverty . . .

In regions such as these are to be found the most desperate ecological, economic
and social conditions. As in many analogous areas to be found in the Old World sub-
tropical belt extending from Atlantic Iberia eastward to Japan, the Persian peasants
of the mountain valleys, no longer as strictly numerically controlled by disease and
disaster as traditionally they were, are presented with few alternatives to dependence on local agricultural resources, and increasingly compete for land and once
plentiful water. Further intensification of rudimentary production techniques can
only mean a greater and more constant expenditure of human energy with an ever
decreasing prospect of a breakthrough to the social and economic opportunities of
which improved communications inform the villagers. The brutal fact remains that
a multitude of tiny regions of this kind are rurally overpopulated except on the
basis of a low standard peasant way of life. No adjustments of tenure or techno-
logical improvements can significantly ameliorate this situation in which the range
of choice is confined to three possibilities. The first is that of migration to the
towns, a practice which is steadily increasing . . . (Bowen-Jones 1968: 576—7).

The situation described here is common in the highlands of the Middle East. The
Tigris—Euphrates lowlands of Iraq however present a contrasting picture.

The situation in rural Iraq differs from that in many Middle Eastern countries,
for here there has been a progressive decrease in the supply of agricultural labour,
following migration from the countryside to the towns. The reasons why
migration continues when the area of agricultural land available per head is increasing are largely institutional. The traditional form of land tenure before 1932 was
tribal, each tribe occupying a piece of land and using it for cultivation or pasture.
The size of the tribal domain depended on the size and strength of the tribe. As an
ordinary member of the tribe the chief or shaikh held his position only because of
special qualities of leadership (Fernea 1969). However, under the Land Settlement
Laws of 1932—8 the shaikhs usurped ownership of the lands by registering them in

their own names. Thus the relationship of shaikh to tribesman changed to that of landlord and tenant (Baali 1969). Conditions became oppressive in the countryside. But the Agrarian Reform Law of 1959, although aimed at destroying the landlord's political power, resulted in further uncertainty and confusion, partly because constant changes in policy and personnel resulted in delays in distribution (Lawless 1972: 112–15). These upheavals encouraged migration.

The loss of the younger and more economically active age-groups through migration created an acute shortage of agricultural labour, with land falling out of cultivation and a fall in crop production. This combined with the increase in Iraq's total population has meant that oil revenues have had to be diverted from development projects to pay for food imports. In addition the physical problems of the irrigated zone have not changed with Land Reform. The substitution of intensive use of land that must be irrigated for extensive use with a regular fallow will cause the land to salt up and result in decreased fertility, unless the very costly process of laying tile drains under the fields is carried out. Without the time-consuming and undramatic policies of laying drains, experimenting with fallow crops as means of reducing salination, reforesting hillsides and educating managerial farm personnel, no amount of confiscating lands and redistributing them to the landless will encourage some of the hundreds of thousands of rural migrants to the city to return to the farms (Fernea & Fernea 1969: 193–5).

Not all the migrants to the largest cities of the Middle East are from rural villages. A number come from the smaller, traditional towns, hence the relatively high rates of growth of the largest cities and the slower growth of the small and medium-sized towns. There are regional differences within countries in this respect. There is a significant contrast between the northern and western cities of Iran, which have relatively high population densities in their rural hinterlands and high rates of migration to the cities regardless of city size, and the southern and eastern cities, in the more arid parts of the country, which have relatively low densities of rural population and low rates of cityward migration, and even net migration away from some cities (Clark & Costello 1973: 101–5).

Migration away from the city of Aran/Bidgol in north-central Iran is a symptom of the population outgrowing its local resources in a similar manner to the rural villages discussed above. Although the settlement, with a population of 23 265 in 1966, is officially classified as urban it performs no specifically urban functions. It is in fact a pair of villages, only a few tens of metres apart, which have been grouped together for administrative purposes. The principal sources of livelihood in Aran/Bidgol were until recently agriculture and carpet weaving. Agricultural conditions have deteriorated in recent years, following a drop in the local water table which has been hastened by mechanical pumping. Many of the male inhabitants have been forced to move temporarily to larger cities, while supporting their families at home. Others have found employment in the modern textile industry of nearby Kashan, whither they commute across the desert. Female employment is almost exclusively in carpet weaving in the home, under contract from merchants in Kashan.

There are few signs in Aran/Bidgol of growth in local economic life. A new road, a clinic and several schools have been built with central government funds, but few modern buildings have been put up by the inhabitants. The improvement in health services has had a marked effect in lowering mortality, and between 1956 and 1966 the population rose by 40 per cent, despite emigration. Population densities of persons per room and persons per hectare in the settlement are high. The lack of growth or initiative from within the community stems partly from the loss through migration of young people, in particular the literate young men graduating from the schools.

## Migrants in the city

The social life of migrants and other city dwellers, the way in which their social relationships are organized, is much influenced by the demographic and economic conditions where they live and by their geographic mobility in the city. Where migrants live when they arrive in the city has been the subject of much speculation and discussion, but closer inspection reveals there is little published research. Among a number of hypotheses about adjustment of villagers to life in Cairo put forward by J. Abu-Lughod (1961), was one which stated that villagers tended to reside near Cairo's rural–urban fringe and in parts of the city characterized by high religious and ethnic homogeneity, high illiteracy and high fertility – places resembling in fact rural Egypt. Also, it was hypothesized that small enclaves of ex-villagers living closely together helped mitigate the effects of transition from village to city. Testing these hypotheses for Cairo K.K. Petersen (1971) found that migrants do tend to settle on the rural–urban fringe, but were not over-represented in districts with highest illiteracy rates or highest religious homogeneity. Rather, migrants more recently arrived in Cairo were less likely to be located in these districts and districts of low socio-economic standing. Doubts were also raised whether migrants from particular villages do cluster in small enclaves of ex-villagers, though few were completely isolated from fellow villagers.

The tendency for migrants to concentrate in Middle Eastern cities according to their home regions varies from city to city and over time. A survey of Tripoli, Libya in 1917 showed that families from the Misurata region and from other regions were living in groups. Later, the Italians rigorously kept parts of the city, such as the Garden City, for Europeans. In the shanty towns which began to mushroom outside the high defended walls built by the Italians there was no pronounced differentiation by region of origin. More recently there has been some degree of concentration according to place of birth: migrants from the desert zone have tended to concentrate in the old city of Tripoli and in a group of shanty towns outside a southern gate (Harrison 1967). In cities as contrasting in size as Cairo and Isfahan migrants tend to live on the side of the city nearest their place of origin.

Until the early 1960s migrants' squatter settlements in Baghdad were built in the open spaces near the city's central district as well as on the outskirts. Squatters in the central district were often helped by urban families who supplied them with free water and electricity. Attitudes might also be neutral. The narrator in J.I. Jabra's tale about an educated Palestinian exile in Baghdad, after visiting a friend in a suburb, says at one point 'with the exception of a couple of black-clad peasant women standing near their mud hut almost a hundred yards away, the street was deserted. No one took any notice of mud hut dwellers, of course. They were faceless and anonymous, like animals which nobody claimed' (1960: 177). After the flood of rural migrants to Baghdad increased in the 1950s the migrants' huts were built all round the city. One belt grew up behind a dyke some two kilometres to the east of the Tigris, even though until 1956 the area was subject to flooding and was crossed by polluted and malodorous streams (Lawless 1972: 120). The dwellings remained until they were demolished in a government rehousing scheme.

By contrast, Tehran does not have any readily identifiable shanty towns, although the city is a major attraction for migrants from all over Iran. The newcomers have been absorbed into the rapidly expanding fabric of the city. The majority of the poorer sort, however, have settled in the southern districts, which are on the desert fringes and furthest from the cooler mountains to the north. These are the districts with the highest rates of illiteracy and highest fertility, and are also the most crowded in terms of persons per room and persons per hectare (Bahrambeygui 1972).

Sample studies suggest that individual migrants' places of residence are often changed. In Tehran many live in caravenserais in the south of the city, possibly moving from one to another. Other migrants live with relatives for a time. Most construction workers live on the building site together with workers from the same village. Their families are left at home in the village. Approximately 50 per cent of new migrants to Tehran who were sampled by the World Health Organization and the Department of Public Health of Tehran University to monitor the health characteristics of immigrants had moved after a period of six months.

The movement of persons to the city and within the city may take place in a number of recognizable stages, and groups at each stage have differing social and demographic characteristics. The stages noted by Darwent (1965) in Mashad can be seen in other cities of the Middle East. First-stage migration to cities like Mashad, or Isfahan, is that of non-established migrants to central areas of the old town. There are frequently concentrations of males living around the old central areas of Middle Eastern cities. In Isfahan and Mashad many of these people are known to be migrants not yet well enough established to bring in their families. They live in the caravanserais and lodging houses of the old town centre or with relatives and fellow villagers. Second-stage migration is that of better connected or longer established families from other smaller urban areas to the suburbs of the big city or from the old town out to the newer suburbs.

Similarly in Tripoli in Libya, migrants in the pre-Italian period moved into the old city, frequently clustering not only by residence but by occupation. Those from the Jebel village of Takbal, it seems, invariably became bakers (Harrison 1967: 400), just as at one time most of Cairo's porters came from Musha village (Baer 1964:

223). Rapid urban growth and economic development in the Italian period resulted in the old city of Tripoli becoming crowded and deteriorating. The city-born as well as the established migrants started to move to the modern section of the city, while the recent poor migrants settled in the old city quarters or in the shanty towns on the periphery (Elkabir 1972: 67–83).

A reverse movement from the shanty towns on the edge of the city into the centre has occurred in Beirut. After the war of 1967 the Jewish community of Beirut, which lived in a quarter near the Grand Serail, diminished rapidly through emigration to the U.S.A. and Canada. Many of the vacated apartments were occupied by Kurdish families moving in from the shanty towns. Where formerly one Jewish family lived in an apartment there were now four to six Kurdish families (Bourgey & Phares 1973: 109).

The types of settlement in which migrants live in Middle Eastern cities parallel the three types of transitional urban settlements described by Turner (1968) and Berry (1973: 88) who were generalizing from studies throughout the Third World. The 'low-income bridgeheads', as they were called, are populated with recent arrivals with few marketable skills. They tend to be in decaying old buildings in the central city or in centrally located hutments, close to where work can be obtained. The 'low-income consolidators' are settlements which tend to be situated away from the centre, and although conventional housing is still out of reach money is available for other necessities. These so-called 'slums of hope' are often highly organized and planned, and tend to improve in quality through the years as residents give money and effort to their upkeep. In the third type of settlement residents give priority to upgrading housing, to education and the quality of services. Residents in these settlements, called 'middle-income status seekers' by Berry, have economic security and wish to seek social status through choice of location.

This division of settlement types corresponds in detail to three types of settlement described in 1972 by Elkabir in Tripoli, Libya. The first, an area called El Hadba, had poor housing constructed from petrol cans, pieces of corrugated iron and scrap, and pieces of wood. Water supply and sanitation were inadequate and population densities high. Overcrowding forced the residents to take their recreation in alleys and vacant lots rather than the home, while high crime rates and widespread prostitution were also a problem. The shaikh of the district, who was supposed to be in some sort of administrative authority commanded little respect. The residents complained of a lack of harmony in the neighbourhood, and tensions between and within families frequently exploded in violent quarrels.

The district called El Hani was not dissimilar to El Hadba in material conditions, but was described as socially more integrated. The shaikh was a source of advice and help in the neighbourhood, and was able to act as a link between it and the city. Family life was comparatively stable and crime and prostitution not a problem. Apparently, El Hani was becoming a 'slum of hope'.

A third residential neighbourhood, without a name, described by Elkabir, is located to the south of central Tripoli. It corresponds to the middle-income areas described by Turner. Residential density is lower than the shanty towns and the housing consists of flats and new houses, some furnished partly in European style. The district is provided with adequate water supply and refuse collection. The residents are comparatively well off and show a high degree of neighbourliness and social participation. They have a lower incidence of broken marriages than either El Hani or El Hadba, and in general family life is more stable (Elkabir 1972: 79–81).

These then are the physical conditions under which migrants live. How they and others order their lives, and adjust to an ever-changing society in rapidly expanding urban areas will be the subject of the following chapter.

# 5. Social adjustment in the city

The demographic event of urban population growth through migration and natural increase described in previous chapters is associated with the process of social urbanization whereby people acquire material and non-material elements of culture, behaviour patterns and ideas that originate from or are distinctive of the city. The family provides some of the best indices of change in the urbanization process; accordingly we shall turn our attention first to that most important institution including the demographic changes that are affecting its structure. The individual is involved also in a wider network of social ties than the family, through kinship groups, tribal and voluntary organizations. They provide the basis for the individual's social actions and play a part in changing attitudes and in assimilation into urban life. There are parallels between the role of these wider social ties in the urban community in the Middle East and similar networks, in sub-Saharan Africa for example. What is perhaps unique to the Middle East, or at any rate to the Islamic world, are the changes taking place in the status of women, given their traditional role in society. Later in the chapter we return to the family to look at changes in the concept of family honour and how this is affecting women's lot. Last to be dealt with will be another field, the media and politics, where involvement in urban life is altering behaviour patterns and ideas.

## The family and demographic change

The character of traditional family organization in the Middle East is naturally tied in with ecological differences between the nomadic, village and urban ways of life, but it will suffice to consider what is perhaps the modal type. This has been considered to consist of a patrilocal extended family living in one household, that is, a man, his wife, their unmarried children, and their married sons with their wives and children. Together with patrilocality were patriarchal rule, patrilinearity (descent through the male line), and a preference for endogamous marriage (marrying within the tribe or extended family). This structure encapsulates the Arab ideal of what a family should be, and the reality did not necessarily coincide with it. It was more prevalent in the countries of the Fertile Crescent than in Egypt (Baer 1964: 58).

Typically, in the urban and village setting the ideal extended family lived in one house or adjoining houses. It was the property-owning unit; and the supervision of the family possessions rested solely with the father, though limited by Islamic inheritance laws which stipulate that the inheritance be subdivided among the children, daughters receiving a half-share and sons a whole share. Among the poorer classes the expectation of any inheritance by the children was, of course, very little, so the patrilocal extended family was weaker with peasant tenants and agricultural labourers than among landowners, large or small.

Doubts have been cast however by K.K. Petersen (1968) on whether the patrilocal extended family was typical in Egypt before 1900 and during the twentieth century, since demographic conditions would tend to prevent it occurring. Marriage for Egyptian males in city and countryside alike is generally delayed until after twenty-five years of age. Given prevailing mortality conditions, Egyptian males had until recently an average of only thirty-two to thirty-five years of life left. A high proportion of a man's sons would thus be born late in his life, and even if they survived under conditions of high infant and adolescent mortality, it is unlikely he would himself survive to attend their wedding. These conditions were similar in the rest of the Middle East, so it is not unreasonable to assume that the patrilocal extended family occurred rarely in practice.

To generalize about the size of families and the size of households can be misleading, since there is no standard urban family or urban household. This has been amplified by Gulick and Gulick (1974) in a study of varieties of domestic social organization in the Iranian city of Isfahan. The Gulicks' definition of a household is that it consists of a group of people who live together in the same dwelling and regularly prepare and eat their meals together. The housing compounds examined were in the old and the new districts of Isfahan. They contained from one to six households. Three-quarters of the husbands and wives in the 175 families in the survey were urban-born.

The size of family households ranged from single-person households, which comprised over one in twenty of the total number, to one nineteen-person complex household; but the complexity of relationships between members of complex households did not increase as household size increased, and it was found that the number of co-resident extended and stem families (in which the members are of common descent) where all eat together is very small. In addition, the situation in households was always liable to change; of the 140 compounds in the Gulicks' sample 47 had changed through the moving in and/or out of individuals or families, in the space of one year. Among the nuclear families (father, mother and children) moving out was a case of the husband, wife and one child moving to Tehran where the man had found a job; the wife's mother, who also lived in the compound, moved with her children to another house which she owned in Isfahan. Among the multiple movements recorded was a case of four related nuclear families, including married brothers and their mother, who was described by her daughter-in-law as a trouble-maker. One of these nuclear families moved out, while the daughter of another got married and left.

Whether in one household or not the members of an extended family in an urban or a rural situation were and are bound together by mutual obligations and expectations. Adult brothers are expected to remain loyal and mutually helpful throughout life, although each may be the head of his own nuclear family. In educated families, for example, elder brothers who are established in a profession are expected to help finance the education of younger brothers if the father cannot. An unmarried girl is considered to be under the direct care of her parents, brothers and other sisters until marriage, when she becomes the responsibility of her husband and his brothers. An illustration of this responsibility when taken to an extreme is given in a passage by Jabra, relating to a fictional incident set in Baghdad in 1948. The scene is an hotel where a man has just knifed his sister to death.

We did not know whether to call the doctor or the police. A tall fellow in bedouin costume, however, shouted to Yousef over the girl's corpse: 'Is it a matter of honour? Well done, man! It's good to see we haven't lost our sense of honour yet. Well done, man!' With the upright carriage of a victor stepping on his prostrate foe, he held the rims of his cloak together and walked away . . .
'And he'll get away with it, too,' Adnan said. 'Don't look so surprised, Brian. The girl had obviously slept with a man, and the outraged brother got to know about it. This was the only thing for him to do. If he hadn't done it he would have been the laughing stock of his family and friends.'
'But she wasn't his wife,' Brian said. 'Surely he won't get away with that?'
'Three or four years in jail, at most,' I said.
'We live in cities and yet we follow the law of the desert,' Adnan explained. 'We're caught in the vicious meshes of tribal tradition. You heard what the bedouin said, didn't you?'
'Love here must be very exciting, very exciting,' Brian said. (Jabra 1960: 45—6).

If a woman is divorced or widowed without children she returns to her brothers' care. These obligations are a matter of family honour, and failure to meet them, if it becomes known by outsiders, is a matter of family shame (Gulick 1967: 131). The wish to preserve family honour is not peculiar to the Arabs of the Middle East; among the Turks of Bodrum anyone outside the family is called a stranger and therefore subject to some denigration. Even women from outside the family who marry into it are 'strangers', who may lay the family open to public shame if they disgrace it in any way (Mansur 1972: 220). Generally there is contact, but with no set of obligations, between a family and its matrilineal kindred, and with married aunts, married sisters and female cousins.

Movement to the cities has tended to break up the extended family household structure where it existed. It is usually the younger generation who make the move, and once in the city the sons are no longer financially dependent on the family property or on the traditional family occupation. They are more likely to be sending remittances back to their village, so perhaps reversing the pattern of dependence. These changes extend also to other aspects of traditional family structure such as patriarchal rule. As master of the immediate family the father pays the bride price for his son's spouse and so has the last word in arranging the marriage, in choosing the bride after discussion and dealing with her family, and in fixing the wedding date. Endogamous marriages, particularly between brothers' children, are still encouraged and sought after, but the practice of arranging the marriage, still common in town and country, is declining slowly. An increase in female literacy tends to go with a delay in the average age of girls' marriage, which is about sixteen, and among the wealthier classes some women can even achieve financial independence through the pursuit of a profession.

The demographic background to social change is marked by high rates of natural increase, comparatively low mortality rates, and a large number of economically dependent persons, whether young or old. It is possible to generalize about urban populations in the Middle East as a whole, but it will be helpful first to look at some countries in a little detail. In Turkey, for instance, differentials between major cities and rural areas are very high, with birth rates of about 24 per thousand in the cities and 49 per thousand in the countryside recorded in the 1965 census (Shorter 1968). Fertility decline has diffused from the larger cities to the smaller ones and so to the countryside partly through a nationwide system of birth-control clinics though, in the small town of Ula, Benedict has noted that those men who knew about birth-control practices had gained the information when in the army (1970: 167). As a result the urban population of Turkey was distinctly less youthful, with 35 per cent below 15 years of age compared with a national figure of 42 per cent (Dewdney 1972: 59). Sex ratios in town and country also contrasted, with 1168 males per 1000 females recorded in the cities, compared with 907 males in the rural areas, resulting from male-dominated migration to the towns.

A similar pattern is prevalent in Iran, with lower fertility in the cities, though it is rising in both town and country; with a higher proportion of young and old people in the countryside; and with a slightly greater preponderance of males in cities, with a sex ratio of 1084 males per 1000 females in 1966 compared to 1065 recorded in the rural areas. Syria, likewise, has lower fertility, a higher proportion of adults and a sex ratio of 1063 in the cities compared to 1050 in the rural areas. Individual cities will show greater extremes. Jidda in Saudi Arabia had a recorded sex ratio of 1326 males per 1000 females in 1963, but there does not seem to be in the Middle East anything like some African settlements where male migrants may be six or seven times more numerous than females, although at times similar imbalances might occur in some of the small oil boom cities in the Persian Gulf.

A close analysis of Egypt's demographic situation by J. Abu-Lughod (1963) questions a number of general propositions which have prevailed in urban—rural fertility differences. It will be useful here to examine in the Middle Eastern context, some of the propositions which have been derived from evidence on North American urban—rural differences, though we must stress that Abu-Lughod's original discussion related solely to Egypt. The first of these propositions is that urban fertility is lower and urban families smaller than rural areas. Egypt's case in particular refutes this, since urban and rural fertility patterns are substantially the same, as are those in Libya and Lebanon, but the evidence is that in Turkey, Iran, Syria and Saudi Arabia there is appreciably lower fertility in the cities. Secondly, death rates throughout the Middle East are lower in cities, contrasting with the North American and European experience during the rapid urban growth of the nineteenth century. Thirdly, in Egypt and other countries where urban/rural fertility differentials are small natural increase has accounted for a large proportion of urban growth; though, as we have seen, there can be a close relationship between migration and natural growth. They are not wholly independent variables.

In conclusion, natural increase caused mainly by declining mortality is of greater significance than in tropical Africa, the sex-ratio imbalance is less blatant and the urban population much less transient. Most cities are old rather than new creations and they have a local core of indigenous inhabitants. These people have some of the same values as the migrants, in particular the importance of family ties, and for the most part they have the same religion, Islam.

## Social adjustment: migrants and migrant groups

We have seen that adjustment to city life is likely to be influenced by the demographic and economic conditions where people settle and by their geographic mobility in the city. Whether the process of migration is socially disorganizing is affected by where the migrant lives, whether or not with relatives, the availability of work and the individual's background and personality. That some migrants do suffer social disorientation is shown by Elkabir (1972) in Tripoli, Libya. The movement of established migrants and Tripolitan natives out of the old city has tended to break the link between established migrants and new arrivals who were moving first into the old city. The process was speeded up by the variety of new urban occupations in government, oil and other sectors which prevented any of the concentration of regional groups of migrants by occupation which had happened in the past. In consequence, Elkabir notes, there was a feeling of uprootedness among migrants, especially the more recent, and many complained that they had lost a sense of community. Geographic mobility in the city has created social discontinuity also in the shanty towns. The demolition of the shanty towns, whether or not accompanied by a government housing project, results in breaking established neighbourhood relationships and creating problems of adjustment (Elkabir 1972: 71).

On the other hand, in Cairo migrants' links with fellow villagers can help mitigate the effect of the move. Drastic change might happen in the migrants' working conditions. It has been hypothesized (Abu-Lughod: 1961) that men may find it more taxing to work as a city manual labourer than as a farmer, though ex-village women may experience a reduction in their work-load. Those men who work in a large-scale factory with a heterogeneous work-force will come into contact with associates from different backgrounds, but migrants often work in the large number of small business enterprises in Cairo, where they are found work by their village compatriots. Some confirmation for these hypotheses has come from an empirical study of migrants by Petersen (1971). Many of the illiterate migrants were in occupations such as pedlars and small shop owners which do not require a drastic adjustment to new work rhythms, and among many of the self-employed links with fellow villagers may be consolidated through their job. Formal institutions, in particular employment-assistance agencies, play only a minor role in migrants' adjustment in Cairo. The most important source of help was contact with kinsfolk, comparatively little help coming from non-related neighbours.

Middle Eastern culture emphasizes personal contacts and relationships and, combined with a system of relationships based on kinship groups, which increases the number of primary ties to hundreds or possibly thousands of individuals the individual in his own community need not suffer anonymity. Indeed for established urbanites the problem is usually how to avoid contacts and obligations outside those essential to gaining a livelihood and those of the family. The desire for privacy which has played so important a part in shaping the character of the traditional Middle Eastern city is carried over to the present day. It can be extremely difficult to trace the homes of individuals in some cities in the absence of an efficient numbering system for buildings and the ignorance or evasiveness of neighbours.

The role of kinship groups wider than the immediate family in migrant adjustment is better understood if we look briefly at their traditional structure. Loyalties to kinship groups which have a common ancestral father, who lived perhaps between three and seven generations before is common in the Arab countries of the Middle East (Baer 1964: 169). Such groups of extended families in village society tend to live in a common quarter; they may have their own guest house, oven and threshing floor, and will, if necessary, band together for protection and security. This kinship unit is called a *hamula* in Palestine, though other names are applied elsewhere. In the pre-industrial urban situation, as we have seen, these kinship groups tended to be gathered together in residential clusters, but residential mobility is now making this less common. It is probable that for most people relations with these wider kinship units tend to be in a state of flux, strengthening or weakening according to the demands made upon them by their more distant relatives and their skill in evading those demands. Where there is some political advantage through kinship contacts, as in the Lebanon, patrilineal kinship claims are extensive (Gulick 1967: 136). With the poorer recent immigrants to urban areas kinship groups may help to strengthen their economic and political position by pooling resources; and among the 'old' families in the Lebanon, poorer members maintain their ties with their richer and more influential kinsmen, more perhaps in a patron–client relationship.

The cushioning effect membership of such groups can have for migrants in the process of adjusting to urban life is illustrated in the case of Baghdad by migrants from Amara province. A migrant usually had some idea about possible opportunities in Baghdad before permanently leaving Amara, either through personal observation during visits to the city or from primary contacts with relatives or friends. Where contact between migrant families in Amara and people in Baghdad was limited, if for example they came from an isolated marshy area with few contacts or close friends, or where they were particularly poor and could not afford to go directly to Baghdad, migrants would move to the capital in steps, sometimes spending years around the Kut region, saving money and collecting information about the big city.

This manoeuvre was also more common among older and less educated migrants (Azeez 1968: 263).

Once the migrant from Amara arrived in Baghdad he was likely to stay with kinsfolk, and then after a time erect a dwelling of reed mats he brought with him from the country. At this time migrants were establishing further contacts, looking for work and learning about features of urban life such as markets and government offices. Some were helped by unofficial organizations based on tribal affiliations that were established in the shanty towns to assist new migrants, sometimes even to the extent of providing pocket money. By comparison with conditions in their native villages there was more crowding in the shanty towns, for a tribe may occupy a wide area in Amara, and the family might have several dwellings. In the shanty towns loyalty to the tribal shaikhs was maintained, despite their role in the past in impoverishing some districts, and the fact that their economic and political power is now much reduced. Members of each tribe collected money to build the shaikhs guest houses, which served as residences, and they even supplies them with funds. The guest houses and the increasingly popular coffee houses where men can meet and discuss the affairs of their own society, and the strengthened relationship between tribe and shaikh which they represent, have actually helped tighten tribal relations between migrants compared with the rural situation. Furthermore, Azeez points out, numerous religious institutions have been built in the shanty towns, serving as public foci for a more intense religious concern than is found in the migrants' place of origin. The connection between religious leaders and landowners has been carried over into Baghdad, and together, it seems, their influence has increased in the new environment. Azeez sees the strengthening of tribel life as a move towards greater security in the migrants' social life, challenged as they are by an urban society which appears to change its ideas rapidly (1968: 281–3). Thus the Amara migrants by the efficienty of their organization may in effect fail to become socially urbanized, in contrast with migrants from other parts of Iraq who are in relatively smaller numbers and who are not so organized, and so have less chance to become socially encapsulated. For them, the adjustment to living in the city may be more profound and perhaps more painful.

The role of voluntary organizations in Middle Eastern urbanization is uncertain. Tribal associations, mutual-aid societies and cultural associations do exist, but the Middle East does not appear to have the profusion of associations that, with their wide range of membership in terms of age, sex, tribe, religion, occupation and social class play so important a role in African urbanization. Not much published research however has been done on their role in the Middle East. The Amara migrants discussed above have been assisted in adjusting to city life through tribal associations. A sample of migrants to Cairo from Lower Egypt likewise showed that about half were members of their migrant associations (Petersen 1971: 570). The function of these associations is to provide aid and burial facilities for their members, who come from the villages, and who pay dues to sustain them (Abu-Lughod 1961: 26). Migrants in better occupations were more likely to join than those in the poorer paid occupations and the unemployed. Petersen mentions also that membership of labour unions, recreational clubs, religious societies and other societies is also less among the self-employed and the unemployed.

It is argued by Baer (1964: 200) that clubs and various associations in most of the cities of the Arab Middle East are dissolving social organization by hamula, though it is much rarer that they affect religious or communal sectarian ties. They may be strengthened by these associations, for in the Lebanon the benevolent societies, run mainly by women, are sectarian in character. On the other hand, Elkabir goes so far as to say that voluntary associations play virtually no part in the assimilation of rural migrants in Tripoli (1972).

## Social adjustment: personal change

Apart from the experience of people in tribal groups similar to those found in Baghdad, how far does living in cities in the Middle East result in changes in the individual's way of life? The answers to this question are complicated by the continued importance of pre-industrial urban patterns of life in many cities and by the necessity to distinguish between social changes peculiar to the city and the general processes of change going on in Middle Eastern society. According to Lerner (1964) actually living in a city is not in itself necessary to the growth of a 'modern' outlook and so to a 'modern' way of life. Lerner's model, simplified, suggests that literacy and exposure to the mass media stimulate empathetic imagination, which in turn stimulates the mental mobility and openness to change which we associate with the modern personality. Psychic mobility is the basic character change that accompanies modernization, and empathy, that is the capacity to see oneself in another person's situation, is the means by which the change takes place. It is Lerner's thesis that a general model of modernization, which follows an autonomous historical logic, may be applied to the Middle East (1964: 61). Each phase in the process of modernization tends to generate the next phase by some mechanism that operates independently of doctrinal or cultural variations. The first phase, physical urbanization, involves the transfer of people from scattered hinterlands to urban centres, which create the demand for impersonal communication and hence literacy. Literacy is both the index and the agent of the second phase of modernization; it is a basic skill required for the operation of a media system. Once a society has over 10 per cent of its population living in cities and has over 40 per cent literate then new desires and satisfactions are generated, and the third phase of modernization, that of media participation, is under way, to be followed by a fourth phase, the phase of political participation.

Relying on data from a wide ranging series of interviews conducted in the Middle East from 1950 to 1951 Lerner has developed a typology of transition from the traditional to the modern personality. On one side are the Moderns: cosmopolitan, urban, literate and usually well-off, they hold opinions on a variety of subjects. A young Lebanese girl, for instance, who was educated in a foreign school in Beirut, identified with and felt sorry for American soldiers in Korea; or another, a great fan of American popular music, was much concerned with the size of the United States budget, worrying whether America could afford so much. A high civil servant in Jordan explained the cosmopolitan demand for variety on the local radio stations.

The musical programmes [from Turkey] are varied every night. They have a different series with a different tempo. One night they have a very nice selection of Turkish and Greek tangos. They are really very pathetic and sensational. Another night they have hot music, jazz and swing. This is also very enthusiating. On another occasion they have an excellent series of Spanish guitars. Very often they have classical music – music of Beethoven and Schubert. (Lerner 1964: 345)

To him, and to his peers, the mass media are an indispensable instrument of modern civilization.

At the other extreme the traditional personality was illiterate, rural, non-participant and uninterested in non-personal matters. A Turkish shepherd was shocked even to be asked what he would do if head of the government; or a Jordanian bedouin, when asked for his opinion of world affairs simply replied that he was interested in news about his household and his camel because they were his life and his link with this world, but he cared for nothing else because he was not supposed to care for what was outside his concern.

There is another group in Lerner's typology, the Transitionals, sharing some of the empathy and psychic mobility of the Moderns, but lacking essential components of the Modern style, in particular literacy. Lerner found that illiterate persons living in cities tended to have more opinions than those in the countryside, while among the latter group those who had a significant measure of media exposure tended to have more opinions than those who did not. The majority of Transitionals were born in villages or small towns, but nearly all now reside in or near urban centres (Lerner 1964: 162). Thus, there appeared to be a link between physical mobility and a change in attitudes. However, high empathy is seen as essentially a personal characteristic that occurs among groups that are sociologically diversified, in a fifty-year-old illiterate butcher as well as a twenty-year-old student.

The total movement of migrants to cities is determined, as we have seen, by regional, social and economic influences, but each individual's decision to move and his consequent assimilation into urban life is a function of his own motives and resources. N. Levine (1973) has analysed two aspects of urban assimilation, participation in urban life and attitude changes associated with social urbanization, in order to combine a view of the broad socio-cultural determinants of migration with the psychological determinants. The migrants studied were male apartment house caretakers in Ankara who, living in middle-class areas away from ex-villagers in the squatter housing estates, should be especially sensitive to any disorganization caused by moving to the city. These migrants in Lerner's typology could be called Transitionals.

Levine found that the older an individual is the less participation he shows in urban life; the more years these caretakers had lived in the city the more new culture contacts they had made, as might be expected, but there was no appreciable decrease in contacts with their home village over time. In fact the more contacts the care-taker had with his home village, whether through letters or personal visits to the village, or visits from the village to the city by friends, the more likely was he to become exposed to the mass media and to develop contacts with people from the city. There is, then, a positive relation between old culture contacts and new culture contacts for these people who are comparatively isolated compared with those in the cities living in tribal groups. Also, regardless of the amount of contacts they have with their villages, there is a positive relation between education and the extent to which they feel adjusted, their age, and the number of years they have lived in Ankara. The level of the caretakers' income and the size of the village where they came from showed no relation with urban acculturation.

These findings indicate that those who have come to the city are already com-mitted to change and accept that they will become city people. It was generally found to be the case that as the individual increases his contacts within the city he changes his beliefs, attitudes, and perceptions of society towards 'modern-oriented' ones, in particular with regard to conservatism towards women and economic aspirations for himself and his son. The caretakers' more permissive attitude towards women contrasts with the traditional urban attitude, which was generally more restrictive than in the villages. Levine concluded that provided there is employment available in the city and the individual was not blocked by economic disability people who migrate from a city to rural areas can become acculturated to city life. which is taken to imply increasing modernity, by increasing their participation in living like city people and changing their attitudes and beliefs to those of city people.

The process of migrant assimilation among a wider range of migrants than those in one occupation has been studied by Elkabir in Tripoli, Libya (1972). Elkabir measured assimilation by signs of modernity such as a high degree of empathic ability, a favourable attitude towards women's emancipation, a low degree of religiosity and the degree of participation and interaction in city life. There are some close parallels between his findings and those of Levine. Elkabir found that the older the migrant the lower is his assimilation in urban life; the more years migrants had lived in Tripoli the higher their assimilation and the lower their age on arrival the higher their assimilation. The more contacts a migrant had with people born in Tripoli, the higher his level of education, and the more use he made of mass media and the higher his level of occupation the greater was the degree of assimilation. Also, comparison of migrants living in the best of the three migrants' suburbs described in the previous chapter with the others showed a greater degree of mod-ernity, and greater stability of marriage. Similarly, Snaiberg (1970) points to the significance of the early life-cycle residential experience of migrants in determining the modernity of migrant women in Ankara city compared with women in four villages in Ankara province.

The conclusions of these studies, together with those of Lerner, tend to show that certain traits associated with modernism are more commonly found in the city.

But whether they amount to a way of life which can be called urban *per se* is
another matter. The conclusions also point towards the possibility that a general
model of social modernization associated with migration and social change is as
applicable in the Middle East as other parts of the developing world. In itself however this does not carry us very far forward in an understanding of social urbanization in the Middle East. We are concerned to ask whether the urban ethos developing is something peculiar to the region, and if so, of what social values, traditional
and modern, it is compounded. We shall therefore look at two aspects of social
change which affect all levels of Middle Eastern society, attitudes to women and
attitudes to the mass media, and then at aspects of change in social groups in
religion, in politics and in some other traditional social institutions.

### The status of women

In most societies woman's world differs from man's world; usually it is more
narrowly circumscribed. What is peculiar to the Middle East is that the differences
are institutionalized. Islam is partly responsible in that, in Islamic institutions,
preference is given to the male. Divorce and polygamy are the two matters on which
Islam continues to exercise a negative influence on the status of women (Baer 1964:
35). The inferior position of women is emphasized by the traditional prohibition of
divorce by the wife and its ready availability to the husband. Most Middle Eastern
countries however now have new laws which make the women's position stronger
and increase possibilities for women to divorce their husbands, and polygamy is now
rare and probably declining. In any case the traditional attitudes towards women are
not religious in origin; rather they appear to be related to secular values bound up
with the concept of family honour (Dodd 1973).

Family honour has been discussed in some detail by P. Dodd for Arab society,
but much of his analysis may be applied to Turkish and Persian societies. Family
honour is an attribute both of individuals and the family as a group, and it is primarily defended by the agnates: father, brother, father's brother and agnatic
cousins, that is blood related rather than marriage related. It extends to a wide
range of actions, such as loud speech and appearance in public, which may be only
remotely connected with sex. The family honour is primarily a possession of the
males and is a matter of reputation even more than of fact. Women take responsibility for the observance and enforcement of the honour code as well. The high
value put on honour, and the necessity to defend it, results in the actions of
women, and by extension the actions of men, being strictly circumscribed. Social
activities involving public appearance, most occupations, political and military
activities, must be strictly male. Education must be segregated by sex. The activities
of women must be predominantly private or subject to supervision: in the house,
working in the fields, visiting, child-rearing. In the pre-industrial city the emphasis
on family privacy influenced the design of houses and the pattern of social relationships at the family level.

The traditional woman's world is thus confined to areas where the family honour will not be put at risk: the home and private communications-patterns between women of several homes. Men from outside the family have restricted access to the former and no access to the latter. In turn, women have limited access to the sphere of earning a living, though they do work the land, but virtually no access to the public sphere of communications (Van Nieuwenhuijze 1965: 71). In a small traditional town like Ula, in Turkey, the women work in the tobacco fields, but they must reach their work only by going along back alleys, without attracting attention to themselves (Benedict 1970). The daily round of the traditional women is summed up in an interview, quoted by Lerner, with an illiterate Lebanese peasant woman:

Asked how she got her news, she replied: 'From the neighbours; at the bakery when I go to bake the bread, and at the well where I get our drinking water. (Who tells you the news when you're at those two places?) All the women who go there. (What do they usually talk about?) About who is going to marry, who is going to have a baby, who went to Tripoli, and what for, who quarrelled with whom and why'. (Lerner 1964: 177)

What a contrast with the Lebanese girl student who was worried about the size of the U.S. budget!

Traditionally, the pattern of relationships between men and women in private life is dominated by the formal authority of husband over wife. This is partly reflected in the authority of brother over sister. Women may have contacts with a limited number of male relatives, varying with the women's age, since as they grow older (and presumably less open to temptation) they see more people. If the husband and male family representatives are absent the wife may, exceptionally, represent the home to male visitors, though in a manner that underscores her vicarious position (Van Nieuwenhuijze 1965: 72). But the unlooked-for visitor may find himself carrying on a conversation by shouting through a locked and barred front door. When the woman leaves the home the protection of privacy is maintained by a veil or hood, or in countries where the veil is illegal by some other drab garment that enfolds them completely. When the regimes of Ataturk in Turkey and that of Reza Shah in Iran banned the veil it is said that some urban women never again left the house rather than be exposed in public.

The traditional status of women as inferior by nature was accompanied in Middle Eastern societies by emphasis on the supposedly masculine virtues of courage, pride and aggressiveness in men. Societies of this kind have been called 'male vanity cultures'. The strongman is a popular symbolic figure in the Arab, Turkish and Persian worlds. Advertisements may frequently be seen in Arab cities for musclemen contests; in Iran the *zorkhaneh*, house of strength, is an important and popular institution, while in Turkey wrestling is a national sport. The seclusion of women is a contributory factor to the frequency of homosexuality and tolerant attitudes towards it (Baer 1964: 42).

If movement to the cities has tended to break up the extended family structure we should expect changes in attitudes towards women, since male blood relations are less likely to be living close enough to most families to keep an eye on the doings of the female agnatic relations who could put their family and personal honour at risk. That this may be happening is shown by the findings of Levine and Elkabir discussed above, that men tended to have a progressively more favourable attitude towards women's emancipation the longer they lived in the city. In addition, it may be that in moving away from subsistence agriculture women cease to become essential units of the total labour force and so may acquire more freedom. As in most things, however, the degree of emancipation achieved by women depends on the family's economic resources. Those who can afford a lengthy education, its fees and the lack of income during that period, tend to be more emancipated. The early reform associations, such as the Egyptian Federation of Women, have been urban-based and upper class. The education of urban Egyptian women has been shown by Abu-Lughod (1965a) to have a powerful inhibiting influence on fertility. The implication is that education provides women with a choice of activities other than their assigned work and sex roles. Education is probably more advanced in urban Kuwait than anywhere in the Middle East, and here it has provided outlets for women in teaching (where the sexes can be segregated, as in medicine), but there are fewer outlets in commerce, where there are greater obstacles to changes in woman's position.

According to Dodd, however, the rapid physical urbanization has not itself resulted in much change in the valuation of family honour nor, therefore, in attitudes to women. He rightly points to the fact, to be discussed in more detail below, that anonymity is not generally a feature of the Middle Eastern city. For most people the predominant style of life is a set of interactions with known persons. Reference to traditional urbanism shows that a model for city life with female segregation already exists in Middle Eastern culture; and the veiling of women is showing remarkable persistence in many parts of the Arab world. However, Dodd bases his view of the effect of physical urbanization on family structure also on a tentative statistical test involving birth rates and a number of assumptions:

Most crucially, one has to assume that a change in the value of [family honour] will result in a change in the birth rate. This assumption covers a complex causal sequence which may be summarised as follows: the valuation of [family honour] implies a set of norms requiring early marriage for all adult women, restrictions on activity, the forbidding of many types of occupations, ambivalence towards education. Associated with these [family honour] norms is the importance of child-bearing, especially the production of sons. The traditional family structure has therefore resulted in very high birth-rates. Relaxation of any of these norms should result in lower birth-rates.

A second assumption is that data on birth-rates are accurate and valid. (1973: 49).

Citing Egypt and Lebanon as examples, Dodd suggests that the absence of urban–rural fertility differentials is evidence that the traditional norms are continuing to be upheld in the urban areas. Even this tentative suggestion however cannot be taken as it stands. Although in Libya urban and rural fertility patterns have remained the same, in other Arab countries, notably Iraq (Jones 1969), fertility is actually higher in the cities. Outside the Arab Middle East, in Turkey and Iran, fertility is markedly lower in the cities.

There is no single attitude to women in Middle Eastern cities, but all have in common the feature that cafes, teahouses, ice cream parlours, where women can go, are usually divided into two parts, with a mezzanine floor or an inner secluded section for families. Males who are not accompanying their family are politely kept out, and the women themselves will not enter unless accompanied by at least one male member of their immediate family. Only in the westernized hotels, bars and restaurants does this not apply. Again, differences between cities are illustrated by Kuwait and Tripoli in Lebanon; in the latter women may go unaccompanied to the cinema in pairs, if lightly veiled, and once inside they may smoke (Gulick 1967: 5), whereas in Kuwait City the cinemas are divided completely into a family half and a half for single men. Attitudes are usually more conservative in the provincial towns than in capital cities, and they vary from one urban district to another. In westernized north Tehran Western-style dress for women is normal, but in the southern districts an unaccompanied woman without an enveloping garment risks molestation.

## Social adjustment: the media and politics

It is generally held that communication, particularly the mass media, plays a significant role in the process of social urbanization. Indeed Elkabir argues that mass media, education and occupation are measures of a general independent variable, namely, communication (1972: 193—4). Age and integration are held to be conditional factors which facilitate the influence of communication on the assimilation of migrants. Education is seen by Elkabir as a particular aspect of communication, differing from mass media in that it has become formal and institutionalized with regard to the clients' obligations and service, it requires the client's participation, and it is directed to a specific age group. A similar view with regard to the significance of access to and use of the mass media is taken by Lerner (1964), who cites numerous cases to show the link between literacy and the mass media. Those who read newspapers, he argues, also tend to be the heaviest consumers of cinema films, radio broadcasts and other media products. The difference in media accessibility between rural areas and cities was a major reason for differences in modernization between countryside and city.

Many of those in the cities who have neither literacy enough to read newspapers nor cash enough to buy a radio or television can get fairly regular access to the cinema. The role of the cinema in transmitting information about new lifeways has been stressed by Lerner, quoting snippets from interviews such as: 'The movies are like a teacher to us . . . who tells us what to do and what not'. 'They portray roles in which richer lives are lived and provide clues as to how these roles can be enacted by others' (1964: 235). Since the date of Lerner's survey, 1951—2, television has taken over some of the functions of the cinema. A small town like Aran/Bidgol in central Iran has gone straight from the radio era to that of television. No cinema was ever established in the place and, now that television transmissions can be received from Tehran, none is ever likely to be.

Although the media are controlled to some extent by the government in every Middle Eastern country it is perhaps possible to exaggerate their influence on life styles or on political attitudes. True, the importance of modern media in political life was recognized early in Turkey by Kemal Ataturk, who built 'people's houses' in the villages for folk to gather in and placed radios in them so they could hear the news. The influence of the cinema on life styles and politics in Amman in the late 1950s was described by J. Hacker as follows:

The film in 'Amman is regarded purely as entertainment. The audience approach is similar to that of the Charlie Chaplin—Mary Pickford era, before the splendid productions of the UFA studios in the late twenties set the critics to discussing the film as an art form. The people of 'Amman are not interested in the film as art; nor in the films as propaganda; nor the film as posing or resolving a social problem. They go for entertainment as formerly they sat round the storyteller in the cafe. The majority of films shown are American, either Westerns or costume-dramas of the fictional-historical school, e.g. Robin Hood or Ben Hur. The film of action is an obvious choice for young men in their teens or twenties who can identify themselves with the swashbuckling hero. It is more easy to understand in a foreign tongue than a psychological film of more subtle dialogue. Slapstick is also popular. Arabic films are usually of a more sentimental type, dealing with love, infidelity, divorce. Documentary films are unpopular, unappreciated, their value not recognised.
    The film brings a short respite to those whose circumstances are dull or sordid, but it has little apparent influence on them in other ways, apart from accustoming them to the use of the minor artifacts of western life. The values and problems of the western world as presented in western films are so alien to the mode of life in Jordan that they pass unregarded. (Hacker 1960: 96)

The author does however go on to say that the cinema and the radio may yet become a powerful instrument for the moulding of opinion and conduct. Further doubts on the significance of the mass media in achieving rapid changes in Middle Eastern modes of thought have been cast by Roos (1968), who found that political attitudes could change in rural Turkey far more quickly than could be brought about simply by the spread of media and education. The numerous unofficial channels of communication between town and country may be of greater significance.

The range of possible differences in changes of political attitudes relating to migrants' status and their path to the city is posited by J. Abu-Lughod in Egypt (1972: 315—34). It is supposed firstly that those who remain as residents in Egyptian villages are likely to develop a real sense of participation in local politics as real power of control over local destinies is increasingly devolved to the village level. So too will those villagers who move temporarily to the city while retaining their roots in the village. The migrant who moves permanently for higher education may enter the highly literate and powerful urban elite who direct national policies or at a lesser level he may find an economic role in the large-scale industrial sector, and so become involved in politics perhaps through trade-union activities. Those, however, who move to the city through military service and then stay may become more or less involved in politics, depending on whether they identify with their home village, their occupation or their workplace. The poorest migrants forced to leave the village by lack of economic opportunity may join the mass of unskilled workers in the small-scale industrial sector comprised of marginal production and commercial enterprises. Such people are likely to remain unpoliticized with regard to national politics and the mass media, though perhaps becoming involved in demonstrations and other mass political activities, or in local city quarter politics in Cairo and Alexandria (Abu-Lughod 1972: 329–31). These are the folk who fill the streets for mass popular events such as the funeral in Cairo in 1975 of Um Kalthoum, the celebrated Arab singer, which drew crowds comparable in size and fervour to those at the funeral of Churchill or Stalin.

Although the process of social urbanization may tend in individuals to be associated with a decline in public religious practice, the reverse may be the case with regard to tribal groups, as with the Amara peasants in Baghdad, or with sectarian groups. The reinforcement of sectarian loyalty among rural migrants in two Lebanese suburbs has been shown by F.I. Khuri (1972) to be a shift from family political allegiance to sectarian allegiance in politics, perhaps as a stage towards national allegiance. The background lies in the nature of village politics, which are largely determined by conflicts between family groups in Lebanon, as elsewhere in the Middle East. When the honour, 'face' or leadership of a family are threatened it acts as a political body. Other families may provide support or act in the prestigious role of mediator. Village quarters however are identified with different factions only if they are inhabited by different family groups. Families tend to be localized within the villages, though there may be class division within the groups of families. Village public opinion is not appealed to by families in conflict. The conflict is kept private, and support is derived from paternal, maternal affinal or even economic ties. Religious sect is an important element in national politics, but it had little importance in villages. Shiite Muslims, Sunni Muslims, Maronite Christians and others coexisted peacefully in the same villages through the polite interchange of visits and gifts and by refraining in public from adverse comment on one-another. Political activity and competition was restricted to family groups within the same sect, not between sects.

A shift away from this situation is described by Khuri in Shiyah and Ghbayri, suburbs of Beirut, which were until 1956 organized as one municipality called Shiyah. Until the First World War Shiyah had a numerical preponderance of Maronites over Shiites, and some unity of purpose united the two in that both were involved in a single economic enterprise, silk production, up to its decline in the 1920s. The ratio in numbers between the sects was altered however by increased Shiite immigration, particularly to a new settlement called Ghbayri, founded in the late 1920s, within the municipality. Beirut's growth and the development of the two communities into suburbs accentuated the difference, as disputes arose about the spending of municipality money on development projects. Eventually, in 1956, the two split to become separate municipalities. The primary factor identified by

Khuri as responsible for the growth of these sectarian municipal identities was a shift away from family to sect loyalty among the newcomers migrating to the two suburbs.

Living in rented houses and working in salaried jobs, the newcomers were no longer involved in the issues of property, inheritance, and irrigation which provoke family conflict in the villages, nor did they now necessarily live close to their own families. The honourable use of the family was denied to them as a means of participating in local affairs, since they would be dishonourably subordinating themselves to the interests of older, established families in the suburbs, and so new migrants participate in politics through public allegiance to their sect. In both suburbs public manifestations of sectarian loyalty, such as the Shiite passion plays in Ghbayri, or the activities of the Maronite Phalange party in Shiyah, became more open during the decades between 1930 and 1950 than they ever would have been in the smaller, closer world of the village, where people heeded their neighbours' religious feelings.

# 6. Occupations and social stratification

The interplay of modern and traditional aims and interest in the family and marriage and in groups' involvement in religion and politics is seen also when we look at occupations and social stratification in the city. The tendency among tribal and political groups appears to be compounded of moves towards party politics, perhaps on class lines, and reassertion of tribal or religious political interests. In the present chapter we shall ask how far it is possible to conceive of the structure of urban society as being constituted from a multiplicity of autonomous but interdependent groups, and on the other side how far is it moving towards a society ordered on lines of class related to occupation and wealth, the type of society that might be expected to result from the expansion of capitalism. Central to the discussion will be where wealth comes from in the city and who it goes to, so we shall first deal with the structure of urban economies.

## The structure of urban economies

The chief sources of wealth in Middle Eastern society in the past were the owner-ship of agricultural land, and the control of its produce through tax farming or commercial contracts, or in long-distance trade. Land ownership has become rela-tively less important as a source of wealth since land reforms have transferred some land to peasant farmers and as more lucrative means of wealth-getting have become available. The growth of manufacturing has been one such means, and dealing with oil and oil products is another. There are striking differences in the impact of oil on state's economies even between such similar states as Abu Dhabi and Dubai, two of the United Arab Emirates. Abu Dhabi was formerly a simple desert shaikhdom, with nomadism and a little agriculture, fishing and smuggling as means of support, while Dubai, before oil, was a flourishing commercial port sited on a creek with a small traditional Persian-style town. A decade after the first production of oil in these shaikhdoms the impact on ways of life was markedly different; Abu Dhabi had a brand new city, purpose built for a modern state, and little else but the desert, while Dubai more readily absorbed the effects of new found wealth by expanding and modernizing the old town, but retaining and increasing its important commercial functions. In Abu Dhabi it is desert nomads who have suddenly acquired oil; in Dubai it is Arab urban businessmen. Both have been at pains to stress their Arabness, however, particularly through encouragement of traditional sports and pastimes, such as hawking and camel racing.

A further possibility for new wealth has been through the enormous opportunities for land speculation presented by the growth of cities, whether through the sale of land for building on the periphery or through redevelopment of the urban central area. Another significant change in the basis of economic power has been increasing government intervention in economic affairs, in particular through progressive nationalization of major industrial concerns like the oil industry or steel making. In one sense the diminution in Egypt or Libya or Iraq of some aspects of private enterprise in favour of state control is not dissimilar to the situation which obtained at some time under the Ottoman Empire. The state also now controls in many Middle Eastern countries the immense resources of land and property formerly endowed for religious purposes. These changes, and the inevitable demand for more civil servants to run the modern state, have led to the seemingly unstoppable growth of bureaucracies. Professional and service occupations are continuing to increase in importance as a means of economic support.

The structure of urban economies in the Middle East can be divided into three sectors, each with its own variety of means of gaining a livelihood, in a manner similar to that described by Berry (1973: 91) for most cities in the Third World. The first sector comprises the unemployed workers of the city's street economy, including street hawkers, the clamorous sellers of lottery tickets, casual construction workers, prostitutes and panders, beggars and thieves. This individual-enterprise sector accounts for perhaps 10 to 40 per cent of the urban labour-force. The nature of their work, or lack of it, is such that they are unlikely to figure in official industrial and occupation census returns. A survey of migrants to Cairo showed that 22 to 26 per cent were self-employed as pedlars (Petersen 1971: 565) and a survey of a group of migrants to Baghdad showed that a high proportion were employed in building construction, in municipal services such as street sweepers, and as porters or door to door canvassers (Azeez 1968: 284). Competition for work is intense and many earn no more than a subsistence minimum. If there is growth in the urban economy, more migrants are attracted in, so maintaining rewards to individual enterprise at a low level. The traditional bazaar-type economies run by family enterprises are the second sector. For the most part this multitude of small enterprises produces commodities for the poor mass-market using locally produced raw materials. The production of luxury goods, such as carpets for the wealthier market, can also provide an important proportion of families' income (Costello 1973). The third sector, the corporate sector, contains the capital-intensive businesses, the government and the professions. The corporate sector of the urban economy has larger economic units using large-scale capital investments, with high levels of technology and productivity and employing people for a wage or salary during regular hours.

The balance between the three sectors is partly reflected in official statistics of worker status. Changes in the status of workers can be used to measure the erosion of the traditional economic sector by the modern sector where this is taking place as, for example, in Iran. Males provide the most reliable measure for intercensal comparison. Employees formed the largest group in 1966 in urban Iran, being 46 per cent of those engaged in work. Unpaid family workers were recorded in 1966 as 12 per cent of the rural work force but were of little numerical importance in the cities. There are differences from one city to another, not always related to city size. Qom, for instance, had 46 per cent of its total work force self-employed while Abadan has 1.5 per cent. Self-employed and unpaid family workers, both typical of the traditional small-scale sectors, declined from 32 to 27 per cent of the male urban labour-force between 1956 and 1966, while in rural Iran there was a slight rise from 62 to 64 per cent. Further, a rise in urban government employees contrasted with a small fall in rural Iran. In effect, the polarization of the modern and traditional sectors of the economy into urban areas and rural areas was intensified in the period between 1956 and 1966, and within the cities the relative size, though certainly not the absolute size, of the traditional sectors decreased.

## Employment and occupations

Any division of the urban population into economically active and inactive persons is to some extent arbitrary, particularly in the traditional economic sectors where the basic unit of economic activity is the family. If the family is engaged in some form of household industry nearly all of its members may work in it at some time or other. Household industry may involve production for a market or the production of goods in the home for home consumption. The former may be part of a large and well organized system for the production and sale of goods, while the latter is largely isolated from any suprafamilial economic system. Snaiberg's study of rural-to-urban migrant women in Ankara province shows that home production for home consumption is more characteristic of rural residents; urban residents have more opportunities to purchase consumer non-durables (1970: 81). Rates of economic activity in the city vary by sex and by age, and are directly affected by the demographic structure of the population. The rates also differ by country. According to estimates the working population of Iraq is 40 per cent of the total, in Libya 33 per cent, in Syria 24 per cent — though it is likely that the number of working women is underestimated in the census returns. In the boom economies of the Persian Gulf on the other hand adult male activity rates may exceed 90 per cent. In sum, the high proportion of the Middle East's populations in the younger age groups and restrictive attitudes on female employment except in the fields or in the home, or in some professions for the educated, means that economic activity rates in cities and villages are low while age and sex dependency rates are high.

How many of these economically active persons are actually employed? Official census statistics tend to give very low rates of unemployment, yet it is generally believed that the lack of employment opportunities is one of the most serious problems afflicting cities in the Middle East and other parts of the developing world. An explanation of this discrepancy has been made by W.H. Bartsch (1971) in a case study of a poor district in southern Tehran. Questions regarding unemployment usually require the respondent to have taken active measures to find suitable employment in the week preceding the enumerator's call yet, Bartsch says, many persons do not actively seek work since they believe it cannot be found or they have little information on where to look. Unemployment benefits do not exist in most Middle Eastern countries, so a person must create work for himself paying a bare subsistence minimum or even accept a level below it if he is a member of a family or household which pools its resources. The district studied was part of a model community of former slum dwellers who had been resettled by the government. Over 85 per cent of household heads and 83 per cent of their mates were of rural origin. The age structure was considerably younger than that of Tehran as a whole, and the economic-activity rates substantially higher. A higher proportion of women and children sought employment to supplement the family income than would do so in the better-off areas. Questions regarding unemployment which did not stipulate active search for work elicited responses which showed that 14.3 per cent of the economically active males aged ten years and over were unemployed, compared with a reported 4.8 per cent for Tehran; and 51.2 per cent of the economically active women were unemployed, compared with 4.1 per cent for Tehran. Self-employment was considerably higher in the district than in Tehran and over 80 per cent of the male self-employed had resorted to it only after failing to gain wage employment. Bartsch suggests that this may be looked on as a form of disguised unemployment. Most of the wage-earners were in irregular employment and it may be supposed were likely to enter the ranks of the self-employed from time to time.

It seems likely that this pattern of employment and economic activity is common to the poorer districts of Middle Eastern cities, especially the large metropolises. The real employment situation for the great majority of workers is definitely better in the cities than the countryside. Any growth, however, in the corporate or family enterprise sectors of the urban economy filters immediately down to the individual enterprise sector and more migrants are drawn into the urban economy, maintaining wages at the bottom at a subsistence minimum. Furthermore, legal requirements for the payment of social insurance by employers may have the opposite result to their intention. Workers in Iran for example are sometimes discharged after only a short period from smaller factories and workshops to avoid the payment of social insurance charges which are required by law for permanent wage employees (Bartsch 1971). For new arrivals in the city, then, the turnover of jobs may be rapid, and the opportunities to acquire permanent employment and skills on the job limited. A continual supply of cheap labour is a disincentive for modern enterprises to move away from the major cities, in contrast to the Western experience of urban industrialization where rising wage costs in the major cities forced labour-intensive industries to shift to low income areas and so spread the effects of growth (Berry 1973: 97).

The occupational structure of each city reflects to some extent its function. With the exception of major industrial centres like Eregli, a steel-making town in northern Turkey, most cities have a large proportion employed in the tertiary sector of industry, performing service functions. The concentration of sales, services, professional and clerical occupations in the capital is shown for Iran in table 1 where Tehran's occupational structure is compared with cities ranking third, twenty-third, thirty-third and fifty-third in size. Agricultural employment in Iranian cities is the only occupational category simply and directly related to city size. The table shows that there are considerable differences between the so-called primate city which serves as the nation's capital and some of the smaller cities with regard to the proportion engaged in professional and technical occupations and those unclassified, but overall their occupational structures are, surprisingly, not too dissimilar.

## Occupation and social class

We might expect the ingredients of a class system in this differentiation between occupations, since occupation largely decides income and therefore life-styles, and is itself largely determined by education. In chapter 2 we saw that traditional urban society was divided into two classes: on top were the ruler, landlords, the mercantile bourgeoisie and the wealthy religious; below were highly segmented agglomerations of workers respectable and workers unrespectable. The modern change from this comparatively simple division has been related by a number of studies to similar processes which occurred in Western society during the transition from a preindustrial society with its concomitant social, demographic and economic characteristics to an industrial urban society, with the gamut of distinguishing features which make up the term 'modernism'. Lerner's (1964) model, for one, sees the shift from pre-industrial to modern society as pursuing its own autonomous historical logic, coloured by culture but basically the same everywhere. More cautiously, however, Snaiberg (1970: 83) warns that one should not carry too far the metaphor of 'modern' man, and so create a new sociological ideal type.

Table 1
Major occupation in percentages of the employee population ten years and over for Tehran and for Iranian cities, 1966

|  | Tehran | Mashad | Masjed -i- Suleiman | Sari | Mahabad |
|---|---|---|---|---|---|
| Total population ('000) | 2719 | 409 | 65 | 44 | 29 |
| Major occupation group |  |  |  |  |  |
| 1. Unclassified | 7.6 | 9.9 | 7.4 | 13.6 | 15.8 |
| 2. Production | 40.7 | 46.9 | 39.4 | 31.7 | 34.5 |
| 3. Agriculture | 1.2 | 3.9 | 3.1 | 6.5 | 4.2 |
| 4. Professional & technical | 9.0 | 5.6 | 9.2 | 7.5 | 5.7 |
| 5. Services | 15.4 | 13.1 | 17.7 | 17.8 | 13.7 |
| 6. Sales | 15.1 | 14.6 | 9.9 | 13.0 | 20.3 |
| 7. Clerical | 11.0 | 6.0 | 13.3 | 9.9 | 5.8 |

*Source*: Iranian Statistical Centre: *National Census of Population and Housing, 1966.*

The study by Snaiberg of Ankara province in Turkey postulates an increasing contrast between rural and urban organization or social morphology as industrialization begins. During the transitional period between pre-industrial and modern urban industrial society there is a change from a social stratification according to ascriptive criteria, that is, criteria associated with tribe, family, inherited wealth, towards social stratification based on achievement criteria. A man rises in life through hauling on his own bootstraps rather than those of his kin. The mental mobility discussed in chapter 5 is paralleled by social mobility. In the transition period, according to Snaiberg, voluntary organizations provide much of the means of attaining the educational and social components of social status. Differences in the availability of these organizations provide the greatest contrast in the access of urban and rural dwellers to the appurtenances of modernism. As a result there is a rise in what are called middle class statuses and an increase in social class differentiation within the city and between the city and the countryside. Largely because of differences in socio-economic achievement between urban and rural dwellers there are differences in rates of change of individuals and families towards modernism (Snaiberg 1970).

On the other hand Jacobs (1966) while studying the process of development in Iran has considered it more meaningful to divide society not into ranks determined by relative access to income or other material resources, hierarchically arranged into three horizontal layers, but into just two classes differentiated by direct access to security and by lack of security. The upper class are distinguished by their natural qualities of courage and leadership. They are found almost exclusively among the members of the educated and morally superior 'good families', that is those related to Reza Shah, and among the 'old families'. The rest of society, regardless of wealth or occupation, are the 'followers' who lack the security associated with political authority. A clearly identifiable middle class in the sense of having common interests and policies does not exist. An economic division of classes is likewise rejected with regard to Egypt by Halpern (1967: 98) who regards contol over the state and the forces of social change as more potent than ownership of property. Individuals form a social class only in so far as they play a common role in relation to social change, says Halpern, and the new middle-class in Egypt is defined by its ideas, actions and careers relevant to modernization.

There can be an overlap of traditional and modern criteria for social differentiation. In Tripoli, Lebanon, gaining prestige and power usually requires advantageous membership of a sect or family, but it also required wealth, the single most important factor. If political power is added to wealth then the individual has the basis for the highest prestige of all (Gulick 1967: 177).

Added to these points on social stratification in particular countries is the discussion by Van Nieuwenhuijze (1965) who argues that the study of Middle Eastern society must be rooted in the classical study of Middle Eastern civilization. The distinctive way in which Middle Eastern society is joined cannot be called stratification in the western sense. Rather it is a pattern of a composite society that would be pluralistic but for the fact that the whole of society, nomadic, village and urban, converges on a cultural core. Islam, the religion that has determined the formative stages of contemporary Middle Eastern society, has never had the same hierarchical world views as Christianity and so provides no basis for thinking of society in terms of stratification. The fundamental pluralism of creed, language, geographical origin, and of descent in Middle Eastern society has not in the past been overcome by integration. Thus, the Ottoman Empire made no attempt to enforce conformity on its constituent communities. The retention of cultural pluralism prevents the development of social stratification after the Western model. The result is a vague, flexible, variable scale of social categories that eludes overall description of its consistency. For the future Van Nieuwenhuijze sees that notwithstanding some important changes in the middle sectors of society that would reflect in the rating of social categories, the traditional structure of ruling elite and broad masses, with some in-between entities of secondary nature, will persist (1965: 9–10, 25–8).

The spread of social urbanization and the reordering of society from the city to the village can be seen in one urban institution, the coffee house. Teahouses and coffee houses were common in the pre-industrial cities of the Ottoman and Persian Empires. They were places where any male could go to meet others in public, away from their homes, on neutral territory as it were. They were at one time purely for relaxation, smoking, chatting and drinking beverages, but in recent centuries some became meeting places for business talk. The rural counterpart was the guest room in a private household, where friends and relatives gathered socially. In Turkish villages, for instance, people normally only went to the guest room by invitation. In the guest rooms of *aghas*, the heads of influential families, and landlords, traditional rankings according to age and social rank were observed, and of course the subjects and tone of conversation would be largely determined by the host. As Beeley puts it: 'Older men do the talking, young men listen, and boys are tolerated' (1970: 479). The more influential the host the greater would be the number and importance of those at his levee.

The public coffee house has now become common in parts of rural Turkey, especially since the founding of the Republic in 1923. It has diffused slowly eastward from the western provinces, where most of the urban population live. Using Lerner's terminology, B.W. Beeley described villages which have only coffee houses as 'modern', villages with coffee houses and guest rooms as 'traditional' and those with only guest rooms as 'traditional'. The coffee house is open to all without invitation and acts as a public forum where social and economic matters may be discussed. In some villages the coffee houses have become associated with particular political parties. At the coffee house it is not age and wealth that determines who speaks and who listens. It is frequented by the more educated, younger men. Although party politics at the village level are often linked to rivalry between family groups, and the visitors to guest rooms may therefore sometimes be identified with a party, the overall trend is away from the older form of social gathering and towards the new institution. The increasing popularity of the coffee house, an urban institution, is thus partly a sign of the reordering of rural societies according to new urban-derived criteria of social acceptibility.

At this point enough has been said to show the difficulty of a class formulation for Middle Eastern urban society. To avoid therefore the problem of applying and then justifying a scheme of social stratification it is perhaps simplest to adopt an empirical approach and describe varying types of life-style among the urban population. The character of life-styles will, of course, imply varying access to economic and political resources and also to some extent varying aspirations. The range of difference in life-styles varies according to the particular town's size and general significance for the national political and economic system.

### The upper income group

The topmost socio-economic stratum in the cities is almost conterminous with the elite of the whole of Middle Eastern society. It is to be found only in the cities, the centres of wealth and power. The group is very small; Iran's elite for instance is known as the Thousand Families; and the Saudi Arabian Royal Family is about 5 000 strong. In the hands of the elite are concentrated ownership or control of a large proportion of the total wealth of each country. First come the men who hold ministerial rank, together with the highest ranks in the civil service. In Iraq, Syria, Libya, Egypt and South Yemen, with socialist governments of one sort or another, these are the only people that could be classified as in the elite. The government bureaucratic elite which Turkey inherited from the Ottoman Empire has tended to try to maintain itself in the face of challenges from multiparty competition; while in Kuwait the practically open payroll for Kuwaiti citizens in the civil service places them higher in status than either their education or other status would suggest (Ffrench & Hill 1971: 43). In addition to the political and bureaucratic elites are, in some cases, the well established landowning families.

 With the exception of some tribal shaikhs there is no landed rural aristocracy in the Middle East. Landowners were a new group that emerged in the Ottoman Empire and its successor states after changes in land tenure systems. Following independence they acted as delegates in the new legislative bodies in the capital cities. The landowners fulfilled functions of primary importance in civic and national public life in the Arab states before social revolutions and they still to some extent do so in Iran, the Persian Gulf shaikhdoms and in Lebanon. Interwoven with these landowning families are large-scale merchants, real-estate owners, contractors and industrialists (Baer 1964: 207—10). There has however been an absence of economic and political conflict between these groups; individuals and their families may carry out both commercial and industrial activities, so that in the Lebanon there are combined chambers of commerce and industry, and in Iran wealth that has accrued from landownership and traditional manufacturing and trading in one case, Kashan, has been invested in modern industry. In the small

Turkish town of Ula however the landowning group, the aghas, who exerted political and economic control and commanded much social deference, have been divested
of their economic powers by an aggressive mercantile group and divested of their
political power by the multiparty system since the Second World War (Benedict
1970: 202–7).

Although members of the political and economic elite who are of national
importance will live in the capital cities, at the lower levels in the urban hierarchy
each city will have its own elite. Kirman's elite is a small heterogeneous group drawn
from all segments of society: the traditional ulama, the landowners and the younger,
usually Western educated, members of their families, together with the wholesale
import–export merchants (English 1966: 72–4). Leaders of local society, they are
unified in wealth, power and influence in local affairs. Added to the group and set
above it are the provincial governor-general and his assistants, who are the
appointees of the central government and who run the city and its province.

The ways of life of the elite are not easily visible, since the tradition of preserv-
ing private life separate from public life is still maintained in urban society. The
wealthy can easiest afford to preserve their privacy. Their urban houses are set apart
in grounds surrounded by high walls, and are staffed by a large number of retainers
– cooks, gardeners, houseboys, maids, some of whom live in an obscure hutch in
the garden. An upper class man or woman will not perform any task regarded as
menial, that is, involving such manual labour as cooking, sweeping, washing the
dishes or gardening. Upper class women, especially the older ones with no work to
do about the house or children to bring up, may throw their energies into charities,
a very high proportion of which are run by women, or spend their time in idle
luxury, with perhaps much gambling in the home. Jabra gives the following illustration relating to rich women in Baghdad, as written by a twenty-year-old upper-
class Muslim woman:

Mother receives a flood of women visitors every Tuesday. From morning till mid-
night they play cards and drink tea and lemonade and talk, talk, talk, like a thousand parrots about husbands, children, boy lovers, girl lovers, you would think the
whole of the Arabian Nights were coming to life in the shape of those fat-breasted
women. Finally they go away leaving behind their gossip, their stories of sex and
money and scandal, hanging over the dirty plates and glasses and remnants of food
and shells of pistachio nuts (Jabra 1960: 141).

A final characteristic worth noting with regard to the elite is its personal accessibility at work. Face to face relations are important and even the most powerful
figures can be directly accessible to the most humble visitor. As an instance, the
governor of Abadan is separated from the world by only a secretary and a desk, and
so too are even people of ministerial rank, though as Gulick (1967: 135) points out,
such people are well versed in the arts of evasion.

## The middle income group

The middle income group includes professionals, army officers, administrators and

managers, small merchants and educated clerks. The size of the group is partly con-
jectural, but in most cities it is likely to be much smaller than its counterpart in
Europe. Taking first the group with the longest tradition, the religious functionaries,
it includes the professions of the religious judges, leaders of public worship, sermon-
izers, preachers and teachers. The former influence of religious functionaries has
been diminished by modern systems of rule; in Turkey business dealings were guided
and commercial disputes arbitrated with reference to a merchants' code of ethics
which has now been superseded by a secular code that incorporates the traditional
principles, but which is administered by state officials. Questions of personal status,
inheritances, and wills and in some countries the administration of religiously
endowed lands are still the responsibility of the religious. Their economic position,
however, has declined since the abolition of tax farming, while the spread of literacy
and secular education has ended religious monopoly in that province (Baer 1964:
214–16).

The secular educated classes have arisen for the most part during the present century. Most of the products of secular institutions of learning are probably employed
by the government. The expansion of government bureaucracies following independence was enormous: Egypt had an increase of 61 per cent in the numbers of government posts in the 14 years between 1940–1 and 1954–5. The prestige of a government post, especially in the capital, is very high among the general public (Baer
1964: 217–18). As might be expected the teaching profession has grown particularly
rapidly as education has been given high priority in every country. In higher education the expansion has led to an excessive increase in the number of some types
of graduate, notably in law and humanities. These expect to be and for the most part
are absorbed in the bureaucratic apparatus. Doctors, graduate engineers and others
with a technical or scientific education have not been produced in such dispropor-
tionately high numbers. The medical professions apart, the prestige of a technical
or scientific appointment is less than a purely bureaucratic one, and this has tended
to slow structural modernization in countries and cities where large sums of foreign
exchange have not been available to pay for the import of foreign expertise. One
other middle income group with influence out of proportion to its size is the army
officer corps. Generally middle class in origin, army officers have been the pioneers
of Westernization and social reform in a number of countries, notably Egypt and
Turkey.

Cities with modern industry have a further social element in the technician. The
personnel of the various nationalized oil companies, educated in many cases in
Europe or North America, form one of the most distinctive groups. Those living in
cities like Abadan or Kermanshah can live almost completely self-contained,
physically and socially, within the suburbs built by the former Anglo-Persian oil
company. Swimming pools, tennis courts and recreation centres where snooker and
other games may be played are provided for senior employees. The Iraq Petroleum
Company likewise provides club facilities for its employees in Tripoli, Lebanon. In
effect both the employment and the life-styles of the foreign technicians who used

to run the industrial plants have been taken over by nationals. Most social contacts appear to be within the orbit of the companies' employ. That sort of recreation facility is also provided by some private companies, particularly where the industrial plant is 'isolated' in a small town, and work there might be considered a hardship without some additional perquisites. In the nature of their work engineers and technicians in industry are constantly in contact with technical, largely Western, modes of thought. Advancement for educated professional men in general may require also a knowledge of traditional literary, political and moral values. Jacobs (1966: 164) claims that in Iran this requirement at times results in the adoption of a non-rational approach to technical problems. Technical scientific demands may be subordinated to the interests of prestige, and non-technical considerations may subordinate professionally autonomous rational decision making.

Comparison of the middle income groups in a primate city, Beirut, and provincial towns in Iran and Turkey will here serve to illustrate that even in such diverse urban environments they perform similar social functions and are faced with the same pressures from the corporate sector of economy and society. There were few corporations in traditional Islamic society; in the Middle Eastern city today corporations, whether government or privately run, are increasingly dominant.

Hamra in Beirut is a district which grew up around the American University after its foundation in 1866. The university and associated institutions have been an attraction for teachers and other professionals and the district is now predominantly middle class (Khalaf & Konstad 1973). The occupational structure of Hamra is largely white collar, comprising clerks, 23 per cent; executives, 5 per cent; with 26 per cent independent businessmen, and over a third of the total in the professions. The numerical importance of middle-class occupations in Hamra reflects the increasing dominance of bureaucratic and corporate structures in the Lebanon. In business, small shopkeepers are being ousted by supermarkets, while the competitive pressure on independent professionals are such that increasing numbers are taking salaried employment or joining group practices. The traditional economic sector of self-employed persons still persists in the district in small shops, eating-stalls, money-lenders, and the like, but it is in a relative decline.

There is no large 'employing' segment of the middle class in Hamra. This lack, say Khalaf and Konstad, makes the middle class economically weaker than its counterpart in North America, though as an intellectual elite, the carrier of new skills and ideologies and the demonstrator of new styles of life, the inhabitants of Hamra influence social change through Beirut.

Comparison of sons' occupations with their fathers' showed that socio-economic mobility from one generation to another was becoming apparent in the district. More than half the sons surveyed had changed their occupation in relation to their fathers; but even so a substantial proportion were following the family tradition in employment.

Summarizing the inferences that could be made about the middle class in Hamra, there is a high earning potential and degree of socio-economic mobility in the district, with a style of life germane to the spread of new ideas and patterns of behaviour, indicating that here the emphasis is on achievement rather than ascription in determining income; but the persistence of the self-employed sector, the continued importance for many of family contacts, and the enduring significance of communal attachments in Hamra as in Lebanese society in general, keeps the middle class here relatively diffuse and amorphous as a social group.

The middle income group in cities or districts of cities which have retained a substantial part of their pre-modern character may be of considerable local significance. Kirman's middle income group includes a traditional group of urbanites and a small number of young literates with some Western education and a contempt for traditionalism (English 1966: 74–6). These people who aspire to independent thinking would correspond partly with Halpern's (1967) definition of middle class as the group committed to modernism. Many of the modern public facilities of the town are the result of pressure from the group, but the frustration and unhappiness which seems to pervade the group results from their inability to realize their social aspirations. The bulk of Kirman's middle income group however is composed of small bazaar tradesmen, master artisans and craftsmen. The city's economic and social–religious life is largely centred on them.

The guild structure still survives in the bazaars of many Iranian cities, though with much less than their past importance. The guilds of Tehran, Kirman, Yazd and Kashan organize mourning processions during the lunar month of Muharram to commemorate the martyrdom of Imam Husein, they sponsor religious lectures and at times organize secular activities such as picnics and meetings. In Qasvin they do not even do these things (Rotblat 1972: 215–16). The commercial functions of guilds are now minimal, since the government now ignores or bypasses them in this sphere. They no longer regulate disputes, act as a corporate unit for tax purposes, or command control of the quantity and quality of craft goods sold in the bazaars. Small-scale bazaar craftsmen and merchants are under increasing pressure from goods mass-produced in modern factories and the sites they occupy are frequently coveted by the outlets for modern trading companies. The traditional urban middle income group still exists, then, but its commercial and social influence is rapidly diminishing.

The effect that the arrival of a more modern-minded middle-class group may have on traditional social attitudes is illustrated in Ula, western Turkey, a small town of under 5 000 inhabitants. Ula attained county status in 1954, when a number of government district offices were opened, each staffed at the top by professional civil servants. Local born men were recruited for the lower ranks and for many of these it was the first time they had any sense of participating in a national society (Benedict 1970: 232). The civil servants' wives, who came with them to Ula, introduced a number of freedoms: they began to attend the weekly market, formerly a male preserve, and go to the Sunday movie matinee; they visited people in different quarters from the ones they lived in and received the locals into their own homes.

Perhaps the predominant characteristic of the middle income groups is an aspiration towards improved social status. This may be achieved through acquiring wealth or education. The prestige that goes with education and an income above the average is reflected, in numerous ways, through copying some of the social traits of the upper class. Manual labour in any form is treated with disdain. College students, men and women, will not take a vacation job in the summer, in part because wages for unskilled jobs are so low, and partly because it is too demeaning. They expect to be kept, and are kept, by their family. At home all the household chores are performed by a maid and other hirelings. The proprietor of a shop will have a 'boy' to wrap goods and carry them to the customer's car or taxi. At the office tea, coffee or soft drinks are always on hand to be served by messengers permanently stationed in a little room on every floor, or on chairs in the corridor. One Tripolitan told Gulick (1967: 145) that he would never answer the door dressed in old clothes for fear that strangers might think he was a repairman or servant.

Men and women dress in Western-style clothes to go out, perhaps to a public restaurant to eat beef stroganoff or macaroni, as well as local foods such as kebabs. Conspicuous leisure is itself a sign of status; so men may wish to be seen lounging in coffee houses and teahouses watching the world go by. In the evenings, season permitting, the whole family in cities like Isfahan, may dress up and go for a stroll to look in the shops and at everyone else, even though the women may wear enveloping *chadors* over their modern style trouser suits and dresses.

The public image may contrast with the private face, as it did in the traditional city. Some middle income homes may be furnished very sparsely by Western standards; whole nuclear families may live in one or two rooms where they cook, eat and sleep, with a low table for meals, a samovar and the bedding round the edge of the room. The moveable goods are little more than could be carried by a nomadic family. Others have money to spend on Western style furniture, tables and chairs, and electric appliances and a high quality carpet for investment. Some are caught in a social round of visiting and receiving visits from other families, for which a display at home is essential.

A further sign of Western influence on social patterns in the rapidly expanding larger cities — except in Libya and Saudi Arabia — is the increasing availability of alcoholic liquor. Alcohol and prostitution are forbidden by traditional Islamic precepts. This accounts in some measure for the lure cities like Cairo, Beirut, Istanbul and Tehran have for the inhabitants of smaller towns. If the opportunity arises some may visit the big city for a wild time, away from censorious small-town talk.

### The lower income group

The urban lower income group includes persons working as wage-earning labourers, some artisans, and the unemployed. They constitute the majority in all Middle Eastern cities outside Israel, and they share the common problems of higher death rates and rates of fertility than other groups, along with higher rates of economic dependency. Literacy and average incomes are low. Most are of rural origin, either first or second generation migrants. As yet there is little working-class consciousness among the group, and nor did it exist in the traditional pre-industrial city. The existence of this low-rated category of half-urbanized population before it began to function as a labour reservoir of capitalist entrepreneurs and industries, and its continued existence, has led Van Nieuwenhuijze (1965: 47) to question whether it can be called a proletariat in the Western sense of the term. The persistent pre-industrial flow of population to the town in the Middle East in the past allowed some counter current. There is no counterpart to the proletariat formed in the European industrial revolution that had no way back to the countryside and was necessarily industrial. He goes on to say:

So much is clear that the unsettled bottom fringe is typical of the Middle Eastern town. Also that nowadays it has assumed entirely new dimensions and social significance. As a typical phenomenon it is characterised by persistence. But it is persistence of a special nature. The bottom fringe as such is persistent: but none of those who compose it deem their presence in the bottom fringe to be permanent. On the contrary, theirs is deemed to be a fully temporary situation, conditioned by emergencies elsewhere. And what counts is the manner to which this supposition is or is not borne out by subsequent facts. Some may make it into urban society, others not. Those who succeed may find themselves either in the traditional lowest brackets, already mentioned, or in the new industrial labour category. Those who fail may hang on in sheer misery, or eventually disappear, back to the countryside (Van Nieuwenhuijze 1965: 48).

Although some elements of working-class consciousness were described by writers such as Lerner (1964), referring to Egypt during the early 1950s, it is probably more accurate to describe the lower income group as a mass rather than as a proletarian class.

The lower income group contains, then, those employed as wage-earners in the corporate sector of the economy and those working in the bazaar sector. Figures for the industrial structure of Middle Eastern towns usually show a large number of small units and a small number of large units: Bahrein in 1956 had 33 per cent of its labour force in concerns engaging 0—10 persons, but these were 97 per cent of the total number of industrial units. At the other end of the scale the half of one per cent of concerns which employed over 200 workers accounted for 47 per cent of the labour force (Baer 1964: 227). The preponderance of unskilled workers in the cities may be accounted for by the proportion of workers newly arrived from the villages with only agricultural skills and background; and until recently the emphasis in education has been less on technical subjects and more on literature.

The lower income group in a traditional city includes poor journeymen, unskilled labourers, sharecroppers, gardeners, servants, porters, hawkers, vendors and the lower echelons of religious and government service. At the bottom of the social scale ascriptive social values place those whose occupation or birth is not only humble but defiling: butchers, slaughterers, barbers, washers in the public baths, mortuary attendants, leather tanners, privy cleaners and nightsoil collectors, scavengers and gypsies (English 1966: 76—9). Street pedlars are a colourful if noisy part of the urban scene. A count of pavement traders in Shiraz showed 344 along one avenue (Clarke 1963: 34—5). The stalls, trolleys, donkeys and pavement and wall displays of these traders clutter the pavements on the shady side of the streets. Most sell one type of article: lottery tickets, fruits in season, cheap consumer goods, toys, combs, belts, pens, carpets and the like. Itinerant traders can make a living in the traditional quarters of the cities, where the women are more reluctant to visit shops and would rather stay behind the house door to make purchases. Agricultural workers may still make up a sizeable proportion of the total work force in small towns. Some are sharecroppers perhaps on occasion growing summer crops for market, particularly melons, while others are agricultural odd job men.

The average earnings of the majority of workers in Amman, described by Hacker (1960) are extremely low, but there is little difference in wage rates between skilled and unskilled labourers; both earn much the same amount as clerks in government and other services, though clerks work perhaps half the number of hours. A study of income and expenditure among the lower income groups revealed an abnormal amount of debt. Hacker puts this down to the difficulty of adjusting from a rural subsistence economy to an urban money economy, pointing out that a population of village origin, formerly accustomed to living on its own land, possessing its own vegetable plot, chickens, sheep and goats, does not readily budget for day to day requirements when removed to an urban environment. This contrasts with the Amara migrants in Baghdad most of whom, according to Azeez (1968), were not in debt. An interesting fact here was that in 1954 when they were living in shanties about 84 per cent of families' incomes was spent on essentials such as food, clothing and fuel; in 1964, after a government rehousing scheme, 61 per cent was spent on foodstuffs, the migrants started to pay for electricity and water for the first time and over 6 per cent of income was spent on travelling expenses. Moving to the periphery of Baghdad, to become suburban dwellers, had its costs.

# 7. Urban form and structure

We have concentrated so far on the changes in individuals and society as a whole which have accompanied the growth of cities. Besides being a social entity the city is a physical entity, with physical problems, which is formed and structured by the society living in it and by its technology. Our concern with the physical city is partly because society must operate within urban geographic constraints, but also because where direct data from interviews are not available it is possible to infer the nature of the social and economic processes operating in the city from the physical facilities associated with them. The location and design of houses, mosques, roads, schools, prisons, factories, shops, barracks tells us much about the society that built them.

The pre-industrial Islamic city forms the physical and historic core of most cities in the Middle East. It was shaped by a society with two classes, with only the ruler, usually despotic, and his entourage above them; a society with few if any corporate institutions and a lack of corporate identity, associated into numerous village-like communities living in distinct city quarters; a society often much mixed in ethnic composition, with family and private life socially and physically kept well isolated from public life. The principal physical institutions were the mosque, the citadel and the bazaar. Street patterns were irregular and the streets narrow, often only wide enough to allow two beasts of burden to pass. The numerous conjoined house-hold compounds gave the city what has been called a cellular structure, which grew and decayed organically.

Few pre-industrial cities were more than two or three kilometres in diameter, so the oldest districts in the large towns now cover only a small proportion of the total area. Limited in size by the fruitfulness of the hinterland, they were compact in form partly for protection and partly because communication between different parts of the city was limited by walking or carriage speeds. Communication links between merchant and scribe, client and shopkeeper, magistrate and criminal all had to be kept spatially short if transactions were to be completed within an acceptably small part of the day. This was eased by the multi-use of premises for work and residence.

In most cities, certainly in all the larger ones, improvements in transport technology and the selective economic growth that has occurred, with a rise in population, in the past 100 years has allowed new, usually rich, suburbs to be built outside the old walls. Modern road, rail and tramway systems have greatly diminished transport times per kilometre and have facilitated rapid urban expansion. Added to the wealthier suburbs in the present century are the spontaneous settlements of migrants. The typical Middle Eastern city thus has three major physical elements: the old centre, new wealthier partly planned suburbs, and new poorer suburbs. A similar pattern is found in Southeast Asia, West Africa and India.

Physically, the biggest differences are between the old city, and the new suburbs together, rich and poor. They reflect demographic and social differences. Populations in the old core areas generally live at higher densities per hectare; they have higher rates of natural increase and they have lower levels of income and literacy than the city average. In the larger cities the polarization of old and new parts has developed so far that recognizably separate town centres have developed beyond the walls to cater for the needs of the new suburb. In Mashad, for instance, expansion to the west of the old city and a lack of development in the east had led by the early 1960s to an almost complete dichotomy between the city's two parts. Land values in the city reflected this bipolarity, with two maxima, one around the centre of the old city, the golden-domed shrine of the Imam Reza, and one in the new town centre where the government offices were located. The rapid growth of Mashad around the new centre rather than the old signifies a shift in the focus of city life from the religious to the secular.

A further way modern urban growth differs from the pre-industrial is in the emphasis on rationally planning the city rather than allowing it to grow of its own accord. This is not, however, completely new. Many of the larger Arab, Persian and Turkish pre-industrial cities contained some element of planning in the layout of major squares and boulevards, as in the sixteenth-century Mashad and an element of 'social engineering', as in Isfahan, where the Armenian community was deliberately transplanted by Shah Abbas at the same time as the construction of new roads, squares and mosques in the sixteenth century.

The formal organization of city space, whether at the scale of the single building, house, mosque or palace, or at the larger scale of the square, boulevard, or the town walls, resulted in the pre-industrial city largely from decisions made by autocratic rulers. Today this planning contributes a great deal to the aesthetic attraction of the traditional city, exemplified by the architectural wealth of say, Isfahan or Cairo, that has made such an impression on European consciousness. Witness Robert Byron, an English art-traveller in the 1930s:

The beauty of Isfahan steals on the mind unawares. You drive about, under avenues of white tree-trunks and canopies of shining twigs; past domes of turquoise and spring yellow in a sky of liquid violet-blue; along the river patched with twisting shoals, catching that blue in its muddy silver, and lined with feathery groves where the sap calls; across bridges of pale toffee brick, tier on tier of arches breaking into piled pavilions, overlooked by lilac mountains, by the Kuh-i-Sufi shaped like Punch's hump and by other ranges receding to a line of snowy surf; and before you know how, Isfahan has become indelible, has insinuated its image into that gallery of places which everyone privately treasures (1950: 174).

But the aesthetic has played little part in the design of modern towns. It is the needs of modern transport in the city which began the present phase of town planning, supplemented by the demand by rulers for grandiose schemes designed to copy the redevelopment of European cities in the eighteenth and nineteenth centuries. Haussmann-style wide roads were built in most capitals during the nineteenth and early twentieth centuries; in the present century the building of through roads has been a priority in cities lower and lower down the scales of size and importance.

One cannot alter one part of the urban system without affecting others. The effect of these roads has been radically to alter the direction and strength of flows of persons and goods in the urban system. The bulk of retail establishments has moved from the traditional bazaars to the new roads where new factories, office buildings, schools have been put up. Where roads have been driven through the old parts of a town there has been much demolition of old buildings, disrupting the cohesiveness of social areas. The rapid growth of the city has often been at the expense of the garden districts that used to surround the city in its oasis. Kermanshah, Beirut and Tehran have suffered badly in this respect.

Yet for the most part there has been little direction to urban growth because of the weakness of planning legislation and the will to enforce it, and the weakness of municipal councils. The problem stems in some ways from the lack of a tradition of corporate city life. The Iranian Municipal Act of 1913 was formulated by legislators who believed that street cleaning and control over fair distribution and pricing of bread and meat were the responsibility of the 'municipality' in Western countries. Municipalities with these powers were established in Iran. They failed, and were dissolved after four years.

More recently, implementing the Iranian Third Plan (1963–8) produced problems in the urban development programme that were highlighted by the Fourth Plan. These problems were common to Middle Eastern countries in general, and in Iran it has been the aim of the Fourth and the Fifth Plans to eliminate them. One such set of problems as regards master plans for urban areas was:

the limited number of specialized and experienced consulting engineers in urban development, the lack of proper statistics and data concerning towns, the absence of concrete regional development policies at the national level, the failure to determine how to implement comprehensive projects in the form of specific executive projects, and the lack of performance guarantees (Plan Organization 1968: 243).

Town and country planning is not simply a matter of building roads, designing parks or seeing that the drains are right; it is part of the political process. Effective urban planning is possible only in a society which has clear objectives derived from a particular social theory, the will to plan, and the power to do it. The need for an ideology that reflects the overall aims of Arab society is stressed in a UNESCO article on Arab cities:

A new urban ideology is imperative. An ideology that does not succumb to the conventional or the ordinary; and does not submit to the traditional or the 'taken for granted'. Ours, in many ways, are unique problems. We cannot just cope with them, we have to overcome them. Creative imagination always underlies revolutionary thinking. Our needed urban ideology has to be revolutionary. Not that it will jump over reality, but rather that it will debunk, scrutinize and mould present reality in order to create a newer reality. Revolutionary ideology gestates revolutionary strategy. The latter should give birth to bold tactics.

It goes on to suggest that metropolitan growth should be slowed down and halted, and the physical and social deterioration of cities stopped, proposing some ways of doing this. The deserts should be settled and as a necessary prerequisite the prevalent value system which regards the desert as hostile, green as beautiful and yellow as loathful must be altered. Otherwise,

our very recent history (after 1967) should have taught us a lesson: land unsettled is a land unclaimed. If we do not settle our deserts, other hungry, overcrowded nations may very well do it by force of arms (Ibrahim 1974: 99).

This has been achieved by the state of Israel. Israel provides an example of goals for physical and social urbanization that were clearly formulated, with the state having the will and the means to carry them out. Let us look at the background: the state was founded in 1948, with a population of 870 000 persons. A policy of encouraging immigration was actively pursued so that between 1948 and 1972 1.4 million Jewish immigrants arrived, at the same time as many thousands of non-Jews left as refugees. In 1948 the economically most important settlements were along the coast where contacts had been fostered with the West during the nineteenth and twentieth centuries, in much the same way as further north at Beirut and Tripoli. Inland was a line of ancient settlements, Nazareth, Bethlehem, Jerusalem and Hebron, that had altered little in modern times. Most important, over three-quarters of the Jewish population in 1948 lived in Tel Aviv, Haifa and central districts, living on only 11 per cent of the land. This situation had to be altered if Israel was to retain a hold on the territories claimed by the Zionist state, so a National Planning Department was set up with the sixfold aims of absorbing immigrants into the fabric of Israeli society, settling sparsely populated regions, occupying frontier regions for strategic purposes and to establish a national presence, opening up resource-rich areas, and changing the primacy structure of the urban system by limiting growth in and around Tel Aviv and creating middle-sized towns as part of integrated regional systems of settlement.

As there were few small and medium-sized towns away from the central districts, new towns were proposed to fill the gaps. New rural settlements were also built at lower levels in the hierarchy, to bypass the traditional Arab distribution mechanism of villages and market centres and set up a separate, Jewish central place-system. The new towns were planned to help shape the immigrants towards the Israeli goal of a social-democratic, technologically-advanced society. The immigrants varied in background from illiterate peasants from the Yemen to rich New Yorkers. All were seeking a promised land. By fostering a sense of community comparable to that of the Kibbutzim, the new towns would provide more opportunities for immigrants to emerge as leaders, and their comparatively small size would encourage more constructive social work and co-operative behaviour between the new Israelis than was thought possible in the big cities (Ash 1974: 387).

Strangely enough, the planning machinery to accomplish all this followed British town-planning precedent to a remarkable degree, though falling behind current British practice of the past decade. The British mandate government introduced town and regional planning to Palestine, first through advisory town plans, such as Geddes' plan for Tel Aviv, then through a statutory planning system modelled on British legislation, with in 1936 a Town Planning Ordnance. A law of 1965 has continued some of the earlier approaches, and provides for particular uses. The planning machinery is aimed at achieving co-ordinated physical urban development through national, district and local authorities. This machinery however, although helped by public ownership of 92 per cent of the land, is hindered by much of the non-government ownership being in the towns. It has succeeded in achieving development but not in co-ordinating or balancing it. The pragmatic approach to economic development adopted by some powerful ministries is not conducive to co-ordinated physical development, and has had consequent deleterious effects on environmental quality. The beach-front development of Tel Aviv, for instance, was carried out by the Ministry of Finance and Tourism abetted by the Municipality, before the Tel Aviv master plan could be completed (M. Hill 1974: 610–11).

Thirty new and development towns have been built or are being built in Israel. They have grown from a total population of 11 300 in 1948 to over 600 000 in 1973 when they contained about one-fifth of the country's total population. The more successful new towns have been in the southern deserts, while those in the northern region have recently lost population through internal migration. At first the new towns were laid out on the lines of English garden cities, with plenty of open space, low housing densities and large private gardens around the dwellings; reminiscent of the British garden development of Abadan, but there water was available in plenty from the river, whereas in Israel it was always at a premium. The desert climate soon turned the gardens to dust bowls:

... gardening was neither so easy, cheap or socially obligatory as in England and the surroundings of the dwellings were not well kept. The loose array of these box dwellings in their unkempt environment and the sight of people sitting outside in dusty yards in their pyjamas among their scratching chickens provoked dismay among Israeli planners and other officials. This was due, not just to over-reaction to untidiness, but to fear that immigrants might be settling down to a private peasant-like style of life. To scotch any such tendency and to promote social solidarity and the influence of communal institutions, it was decided to build new towns at a much higher density of about sixty dwellings per hectare, mostly in four-storey blocks of flats.

The massed rectangular blocks do express an unequivocal message of the order, discipline and functionalism of modern life. The message is especially stern to immigrants who have come to take refuge in the land of their fathers, where there are very few towns (Jerusalem above all) which have a visible Jewish past on which to build the Jewish future. The 'new' towns of Beersheba, Arad, Dimona, Ashdod and Ashkelon are all mentioned in the Old Testament but they are now monuments to the international machine age (Ash 1974: 389).

New town development in Israel has now largely lost momentum. European and North African ethnic groups in towns throughout Israel are increasingly involved in social clashes, and there is continued migration up the size-hierarchy of urban settlements, with ever more concentration around the Jerusalem urban region. A number of the new towns are in fact more the character and size of a large village than a town and are unlikely to grow much in the foreseeable future. Indeed, the economic and social costs of maintaining them are begrudged by many. The role of some is now simply as staging posts for new immigrants to establish themselves before moving to the metropolis (Sarly 1974). In short, the social role and economic function of these intermediate stages in the urban hierarchy is becoming irrelevant in a country where 80 per cent of the people live in four urban centres.

Although the social forces which shape the Middle Eastern city provide examples of markedly different urban ecologies to those of cities in the industrial West, the techniques developed to study the internal spatial structure of Western cities may be appropriate in this new setting. Approaches to the study of urban spatial development in West European and North American cities, where authoritarian socialist regimes do not place their own peculiar stamp on the form of the city, may be divided into those associated with the study of urban ecology, much used by sociologists, and those associated with the study of urban land economics and central-place theory, the theory of the location, size, nature and spacing of places that serve as market centres for regional communities by providing them with goods and services, though in practice these approaches overlap. Examples of the application of each of these to the urban social geography of the Middle East will be examined below.

Two practical considerations have influenced analyses of urban social space. Firstly, though frequently difficult to obtain, census tract data are becoming available for a growing number of Middle Eastern cities. With such data it is possible to map patterns of human ecological variables in much greater detail than was possible using the often intuitive insights of earlier field researchers. But, as with the use of such data in Western cities, it is by no means certain that these inductive methods will produce better generalizations about the spatial patterning of society. Secondly, a reaction to the great mass of data has been provided by what is called gradient analysis, which is based on the notion that many features of a city tend to vary in logical sequence at increasing distances from the centre. Variations arising from distance from the centre may be reduced to relatively simple mathematical statements and shown in graphs, thus making it possible to compare different cities. Population density, for example, when measured as persons per hectare, appears in the vast majority of cities, Western and non-Western, to decline in a gradient with distance from the city centre. The angle of the gradient and changes in it over time may be measured and compared city to city. The same technique may be applied to other economic and social features. Discussion of the city of Kashan will provide an illustrative example of the application of some of these techniques and the insights they provide into a comparatively small city, as well as emphasizing that at different size and functional levels the organization of urban social space may vary considerably.

*Kashan*

Kashan, located 250 kilometres south of Tehran on the margins of Iran's central plateau, is a city internationally renowned for the excellence of its hand-woven carpets. Much of Kashan's present wealth, however, comes from modern machine-made textiles. The population in 1966 was recorded as 58 468, but there has been comparatively little immigration to Kashan from the local rural area, despite the rapid economic development and high rates of employment which have resulted from the growth of the modern textile industry. Most of the city's 27 per cent increase in population between 1956 and 1966 came from growth of the indigenous population.

Prior to this growth Kashan's traditional quarters were a confusion of twisting alleyways, arches and dead-ends, with numerous household courtyards. Movement from one part of the city to another remained difficult until the early 1960s when modern roads were driven through its length and breadth. Within this largely pre-industrial city there was, before modern growth, a social gradient from the south and west to the eastern districts, revealed by detailed study of the household compounds using aerial photographs and by interviewing the inhabitants. The more spacious and desirable districts with more gardens and a cleaner, more plentiful water supply were upslope in the southern and western parts of the city, while downslope to the east were less well-endowed districts with fewer gardens and higher densities of population per hectare. We may infer from this that Kashan's pre-industrial quarters were not necessarily all mixtures of rich and poor living cheek by jowl because they had common tribal origins or worked at common trades. Pre-industrial, that is, pre-twentieth century, Kashan was relatively homogeneous, racially and religiously, with only a small Jewish community among the Persian Shiite Muslim majority. The wealth and reputation of the family influenced where people lived in the city. One of the most important families involved in the manu-facture of hand-woven carpets, the Borujerdis, had their house right up against the wall in the south-western corner of the city; a prime site, where water from the underground aqueducts that supplied Kashan was at its cleanest and most plentiful.

Population growth and economic expansion from the 1950s onwards resulted in changes in this pattern. To the north and west of the city, outside the walls, several deep wells were sunk to provide a new water supply initially for agriculture, but later for the wealthy suburban houses constructed there. To the south and east cemeteries and gardens were overbuilt as poorer suburbs developed, occupied in the south mostly by migrants.

The accompanying figure goes some way to showing how this pattern of growth is reflected in key variables in Kashan's ecology. The data relate to twenty-six enumeration districts, delimited for the statistical purpose of the 1966 census rather than with regard to social areas. Of particular interest is the contrast shown between population densities per room and per hectare. The former may be more significant in urban conditions than the simple man/land ratio. It can be seen from the figure that densities per hectare and per room are highest in the easternmost quarter, called Poshte Mashad. The quarter is sandwiched between two cemeteries and the ruins of some old caravansarais and is surrounded on three sides by the city wall. Poshte Mashad, like other quarters, has its own social identity; kinship ties are close and the residents speak with a distinctive accent. Fertility is high in the district and rates of literacy are low. The physical limitations imposed by the walls and cemeteries and an administrative order that the area between the wall and the railway be reserved for recreation have discouraged physical expansion of the quarter, and because of close social ties few had moved out by the late 1960s. By then the rate of natural increase and densities per room were among the highest in the city, but by 1973 the area to the south east of the city was rapidly filling with houses.

The central districts of Kashan around the bazaar present a different picture. These were, and to a large extent still are, the commercial heart of the city. Here population densities per hectare are high, but the dwellings are often multi-storied, with many rooms, including perhaps workrooms, and densities per room are there-fore low. A feature of the bazaar area is the large number of adolescent males who live close to their work in the shops and small craft-textile workshops near the city centre. South and west of the bazaar are districts with lower fertility and a more aged population. It was in these districts that, before they moved to the suburbs, many of the houses of the wealthier citizens were found, scattered among houses of the humbler sort.

These suburbs are still limited in extent. In 1966 they contained less than 20 per cent of the population. Densities per hectare are lower throughout. People living in the southern suburbs are mostly immigrants living at high densities per room. By contrast, the northern suburbs are inhabited by Kashan's monied class, and at the western end of the northern boulevard, nicknamed 'Kashan's Persepolis', are the most opulent houses, inhabited by the city's leading bureaucrats, industrialists and carpet-nabobs.

The need to look at several variables in the ecology of the city becomes apparent if we look further at just these two variables relating to population density. Taking the city as a whole densities of population per hectare show a clear contrast between the old town and the new suburbs, and in fact this index has close associations with other indices of housing type and density, such as the persons-per-room index and the proportion of dwellings built of mud and brick in each enumeration district. Though densities per hectare and per room are associated their distributions are not the same. Whereas the former index highlights differences between the old and the new quarters, the latter is related positively to distance to the city centre. In other words, the further from the old city centre the greater are the densities of persons per room. With regard to densities per room at any rate, Kashan is the exact opposite of most cities studied in both the western and non-western world.

Kashan does indeed show the expected contrast between the old town and the new town in some respects, but there are residual elements of a pre-industrial social gradient in the old city, and the contrast between the northern and western suburbs

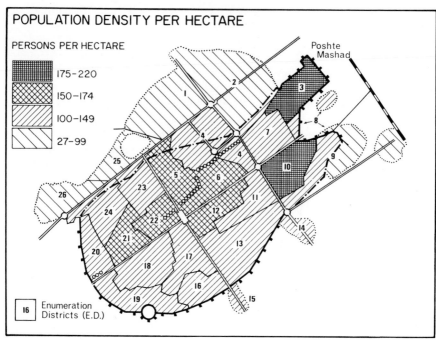

POPULATION DENSITY PER HECTARE

PERSONS PER HECTARE

175-220
150-174
100-149
27-99

Poshte Mashad

1 2 3 4 5 6 7 8 9 10 11 12 13 14 15 16 17 18 19 20 21 22 23 24 25 26

16 Enumeration Districts (E.D.)

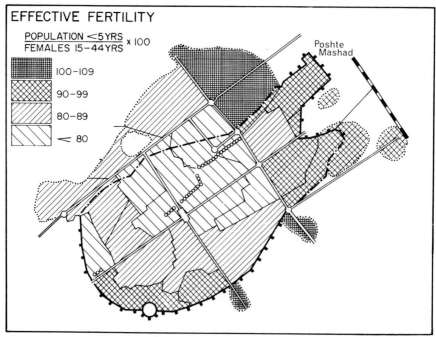

EFFECTIVE FERTILITY

$$\frac{\text{POPULATION} < 5\,\text{YRS}}{\text{FEMALES } 15-44\,\text{YRS}} \times 100$$

100-109
90-99
80-89
< 80

Poshte Mashad

3. Selected demographic variables in Kashan, Iran

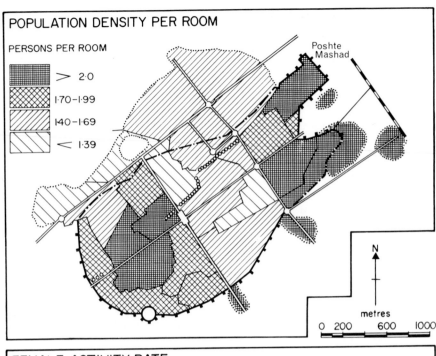

## POPULATION DENSITY PER ROOM

PERSONS PER ROOM

> 2·0

1·70–1·99

1·40–1·69

< 1·39

Poshte Mashad

N

metres

0  200    600    1000

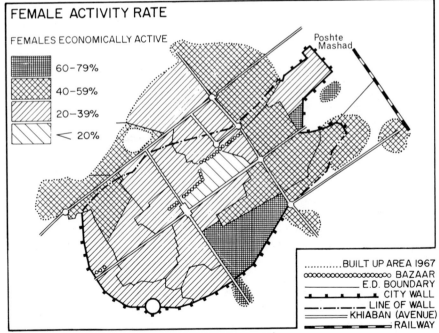

## FEMALE ACTIVITY RATE

FEMALES ECONOMICALLY ACTIVE

60–79%

40–59%

20–39%

< 20%

Poshte Mashad

............ BUILT UP AREA 1967
ooooooooooooooooooo BAZAAR
——————— E.D. BOUNDARY
╼╼╼╼╼╼ CITY WALL
—·—·—·— LINE OF WALL
═══════ KHIABAN (AVENUE)
▬▬▬▬ RAILWAY

(by permission of the Institute of British Geographers)

and those to the south and east may in one sense be only the latest ramification of a social order already in existence. The contrast between the city's elite and the rest of urban society is as traceable in the urban social geography in the town today as it was in the past.

## Cairo

Cairo is by far the largest city in the Middle East and as the capital of the most populous Arab state it is a city of world importance. Apart from its present size several aspects of the city's development stand out: it was among the earliest of cities to begin expansion beyond the pre-industrial core, there has been little effective planning for most of the city, and although a city of great age (it celebrated its 1000th anniversary in 1969), as a physical entity most of it was built only yesterday.

Medieval Cairo, described above in chapter 3, remained much the same in morphology and social structure until the early nineteenth century, when the reforming ruler, Muhammed Ali, who was much impressed by Western thinking, began cleaning up the city, draining local marches and clearing refuse heaps. His grandson Ismail spent, indeed overspent, the revenue derived from cotton exports during the American Civil War on creating as a showpiece of Egyptian progress and enlightenment a new quarter to the west and southwest of the medieval city. While the pattern of life in the old city continued much as before, with craft-based industry, personalized commerce, Islamic rules for commerce and daily life, the pattern of life in the new quarter, Ismailiyah, was European upper-class, with spacious villas served by an army of menials, with carriage roads, railways, electricity, piped water, and an opera house where Verdi's *Aïda* was premiered to mark the opening of another Western technical marvel, the Suez Canal. Ismailiyah was Cairo's equivalent of imperial New Delhi tacked on to Old Delhi. In 1917 foreigners constituted more than 10 per cent of Cairo's population of 800 000. Following the First World War however, foreign control diminished somewhat, and as indigenes began to take over the functions of foreigners in business, technology, administration and the army, middle-class and working-class zones for Egyptian residents expanded rapidly.

As the new semi-elite of Egyptian professionals grew in number many of them began to move to the suburbs from the old centre. Their place was filled by rural migrants whose numbers increased steadily between the world wars. This process of succession is a familiar feature of Middle Eastern cities; it parallels processes of ecological succession observed in most Western cities and is accompanied by ever-rising densities of population around the old city centre and usually a decay in the quality of housing. All the while new jerry-built suburbs were expanding, to encompass eventually the Islamic pre-industrial core and its nineteenth-century colonial appendage. However, the gross differences in life-style between the elite and the rest of the city were largely obliterated by the Revolution of 1952, and in 1956 when royalty and most of the foreigners were driven out. Thus, 'If Cairo is no longer so elegant in certain quarters as she was twenty years ago, she is not nearly so destitute and pathetic in others' (Abu-Lughod 1969: 105).

By 1960 Cairo's population had grown to nearly three and a half million persons, a quarter of whom were compressed into the oldest districts, another quarter in the newer nineteenth-century districts to the west of the old core, and fully half in vast sprawling suburbs to the north. The economic structure supporting all these people was a mixture of corporate large-scale businesses and small-scale bazaar units. The latter helped sustain traditionalism in the city economy, the direct descendants of pre-industrial urban economic organization. The huge numbers of migrants in the city from rural areas provided a third social dimension, helping to maintain rural ways of life even near the centre of the city.

The different styles of life to be found in the city and partly associated with these economic structures have been labelled rural, traditional urban, and modern. These represent the sum of differences in income, occupation, housing quality, place of birth, values, patterns of social relations. At the present time these life-styles correlate roughly with socio-economic status. But direct statistical evidence of where these styles of life are to be found in Cairo is not available, so other variables that are available, notably literacy, the marriage age of women, fertility, and persons per room must be used as indicators (Abu Lughod 1969: 175).

As might be expected census tracts in Cairo that have the highest rates of literacy, a later average age for women marrying, lower fertility and few persons per room, are the modern portions of the city. They contained 16 per cent of the population in 1960. Districts like Bab al-Hadid and the Silver Coast have houses, shops and offices after the styles prevalent in new wealthy suburbs the world over. The people are literate and well educated, work in the modern, corporate sector of the economy, marry later and usually have smaller families than average. At the other end of the spectrum were districts that in 1960 were mainly rural in character, for the most part on the fringes of the city, containing 14 per cent of the population. Housing styles were more akin to those of a village than a major metropolis, there were few retail outlets, since the buying power of the people was so poor, and most of the girls were married by sixteen and had large families; schooling and literacy were low. These areas were being rapidly diminished by the late 1960s by the encroachment of other land uses.

The remaining 70 per cent of Cairenes lived in 1960 in areas where neither modern urban nor rural life-styles were dominant, some 30 per cent in the traditional urban core, and 40 per cent in mixed traditional and modern districts. The lower middle class living in these districts are undergoing perhaps the most drastic readjustment of any social group. It is probably reasonable to equate them with Lerner's Transitionals. Those living in the upper class and upper middle class areas have arrived at some sort of modern urban style of life, while those in the rural city districts have not even started. The movement is in the middle.

The pattern of 1960, which reflected something of the recent history of Cairo, is now changing rapidly, in particular the two extremes of urban and rural society are tending to disappear. The modern city is no longer dominated by foreigners, isolated from the poorer Egyptians. The purely rural enclaves have gone from the centre and are fast vanishing on the periphery. To some extent, helped by the socialist aims of the Egyptian government, the population is becoming an amalgam. This contrasts with the mosaic culture of the Lebanon, where the number of parallel and distinc-tively different life-styles in Beirut, in the absence of a socialist ideology, do not look like amalgamating, and are currently in open conflict.

Cairo should not be accepted as a model for all Egyptian cities. The lack of social differentiation compared with North American cities is not found in Alexandria, Egypt's second largest urban area. Religious groups in Alexandria are located in clusters associated with social status. The Coptic, Jewish and foreign-Christian popu-lations are each in recognizable groups. The foreign-born population has managed to retain its residence mostly in the centre of the city, despite all the vicissitudes of the post-independence era (Abdel-Latif 1970).

## Beirut

Beirut's historic core was, as in Cairo, a pre-industrial Islamic walled city. In the course of the later decades of the nineteenth century the influx of Christian Europeans and the growth of European-style suburbs on the edge of the Muslim city, with the establishment later of the American University in the suburb of Ras Beirut changed the overall character of Beirut. The shanty towns of rural migrants and of refugees were added in the first half of the present century. Apart from the shanty towns, in which there are a great variety of ethnic and religious groups, and the old core of the city, there are three identifiable urban sub-cultures in Beirut. There is Achrafieh, a middle- and upper-class Christian residential district, where the people have Francophile leanings in life-style and culture, and live mostly in large residential mansions; there is Basta, a middle- and lower-class Sunni Muslim district with tradition-oriented inhabitants; and in contrast to these relatively homogeneous residential quarters is Ras Beirut, especially Hamra, a rapidly developing cosmo-politan district. The main element here is middle-class and Anglo-Saxon in life-style. The socio-economic profile of Hamra has been touched on above; our present con-cern is to discuss Hamra's transformation from market gardening to tower blocks in eighty years, through the ecological process of invasion and succession, increasing density and changes in land-use described by Khalaf and Konstad.

Hamra measures only about 1000 metres by 600 metres, so we should not try to compare it with Cairo or even Kashan. It has grown without deliberate planning or urban zoning, in response to free-market forces. Appropriately, the physical features and quality of life are stamped with the character of the American University. This was founded in 1866 in an area devoted to garden-farming, originally scattered with about thirty farmhouses, square flat-roofed one-storied sandstone buildings. Shortly the teachers and workers at the University began to buy plots and erect two- and three-storied red-tiled suburban villas with elaborate façades and balconies. The farmhouse and the villa continued as the most common form of dwelling until the end of the Second World War, when the demand for floor-space increased as waves of new population groups moved in, usually from outside Beirut. The emerging urban middle class, however, continued dominant in Hamra.

From this time onward urban succession, that is the replacement of one urban land-use or social group by another, became apparent. The proportion of non-residential land-use grew as demand by offices increased. Residential development became more intensive: apartment houses of four to seven floors became typical. The remnants of land-use types before the University's founding began to disappear altogether, as walled gardens and agricultural plots were built upon. Land values rose with the height of buildings and speculation in real estate. The corporate sector or Beirut's economy has continued to expand. Its demand for ever larger offices, and the availability of massive capital sums has led to the high-rise building, which accounted in the early 1970s for 22 per cent of all buildings and 57 per cent of the total floor area.

Most (62 per cent) of the floor space is used for residences, but of the rest 18 per cent is now used for retailing, 9 per cent for offices and 11 per cent institutional, administrative and industrial uses. The place is beginning to look like Manhattan on the Mediterranean. What distinguished Hamra from a typical Western central-urban area however is the absence of specialization in land-uses. A high-rise building may adjoin a cultivated garden plot. The tall building may have a bar, or a warehouse or a garage in the basement, perhaps a cafe or cinema on the ground floor, retail and office uses on the next couple of floors, and residences above that. There is thus considerable vertical sorting of uses.

There is little clear segregation in the location and quality of housing in Hamra. The population is largely middle class; many work locally. Nearly 80 per cent of the families consist of parents, children and are occasionally extended to include kin. The great bulk of them live in rented accommodation. The demographic profile shows a low dependancy-ratio, low fertility and a mainly young and economically active population. White-collar and middle-class occupations are the most common.

## Kuwait

Kuwait provides an example of a dual city; with an old core and new suburbs which have grown very rapidly very recently, governed by rigorous planning-controls. The old town was a compact sea-oriented settlement located on Kuwait Bay. About eight square kilometres in extent, it was surrounded by a mud wall pierced by four gates. The wall was built in a great hurry in 1920 when the city was threatened by Ikhwan rebels from Saudi Arabia. The city's morphology was typical of the desert Middle East:

Its courtyards were centres for family socialisation, industry and relaxation. A balance had been achieved — the sort of balance of the medieval city — between man and man, man and God, man and nature, and man and his antagonists: the sea, the desert, the heat, the absence of fresh water, the hard sandstorms. This was the urban and social setting as oil bombarded the city with a plethora of problems (Shiber 1967: 170).

It was a classless, Arab society, largely isolated from direct contact with non-Arabs and even fellow Arabs to the north and west. Absence of class divisions was due to the small size of the city and the intimacy of social contact, the absence of agriculture and therefore of landownership, and the overriding importance of tribal tradition and family pride which prevented money from entering much even into marriage settlements. Apart from the presence of the ruler's palace, there was no spatial differentiation of society in the city.

Oil has produced a class society based on natural origins and income in the course of only a quarter of a century. Money was first infused into the private sector of the economy by the Government Land Purchase scheme, whereby Kuwaiti citizens were offered deliberately inflated prices for land in the old city, thus giving them some working capital, encouraging movement to the new suburbs and allowing wholesale reconstruction of the old city. In 1952 a Master Plan for the city of Kuwait was produced; through the plan the Government established a spatial segregation of Kuwaitis and non-Kuwaitis, their citizenship status being defined by a law of 1948. Only Kuwaitis were transferred to the new neighbourhoods outside the walls. Immigrants continued to move into the old centre, with the result that Kuwait has a dualism in population and social structure that has continued to the present day.

The immigrants were, as we have seen, of mixed origins and fulfilled a variety of functions in the Kuwait economy. The Government spent generously on hiring consultants, technicians and contractors, and facilitated the entry of a large number of workers to help build the new Kuwait. There were also large numbers of illegal, mostly poor, immigrants attracted by the possibility of employment. The city may be divided into three groups of social area: the Old City and other areas of immigrant invasion, distinguishing between areas with both high and low status immigrants, and those occupied by higher-status immigrants, British, American and Jordanian, for instance; the second group of areas comprises those under construction, occupied by low-status immigrant manual workers, mostly in the building industry, living on building sites; and lastly, strongly Kuwaiti areas (Hill 1969).

Naturally this segregation has created its own set of problems. Kuwait City is flanked by workers' towns — homogeneous clusters of Iraqis, Saudis, Palestinians, Indians, Egyptians and Pakistanis. Relative to the Kuwaitis, they are poor, and when ethnicity and poverty combine in high-density urban areas the situation is potentially explosive (Ibrahim 1974: 93). Learning from Kuwait's experience of the bitterness felt now by many non-citizens, Abu Dhabi at the other end of the Gulf has encouraged immigrants to hope that they will, if Arab, eventually become citizens.

Another major priority of the Master Plan of 1952 was to accommodate the car, especially the large and powerful car. The city walls were pulled down and in the old city and the new suburbs wide streets and traffic circles appeared apparently over-night. 'Space, cars, villas, highways, and large buildings replaced the intimate vista, the courtyard, the domain of man, the human scale. The car became glorified until now it is the urban master.' Demolition of many fine traditional houses in the old city has met with criticism, particularly since they have often been replaced with mediocre examples of contemporary architecture. Wide roads, open spaces and the extensive use of bare concrete in the new neighbourhoods give an austere impression. Some of the earlier new buildings, walled with glass, were perhaps designed by friends of the manufacturers of air conditioners: 'the architect who builds such a solar furnace in Kuwait or Riyadh, for example, and then brings in a vast refriger-ation plant to make it habitable is unnecessarily complicating the problem and is working below the standards of contemporary architecture' (Fathy 1973: 331).

Each of the Kuwaiti neighbourhoods has its own schools, shops and mosques, centrally located. The wealthiest modern villas have windows on the outside of the building, giving them an outward-looking character quite the opposite of the tra-ditional house. Nonetheless traditional notions of private housing survive, in part at least, in the high wall that surrounds each house, which gives a sense of self-containedness to each plot; and, in the absence of a sidewalk in most of suburban Kuwait, there is a sort of dusty no man's land between houses and the road.

## Tehran

It is not always necessary to use complicated statistical techniques to see social vari-ations from one part of the city to another. A social gradient on the grand scale can be seen on the ground in Tehran, where a transect walked from one end of the city to another shows the interplay between site, climate, situation, and the nature of the society that has used them. It can be done by any hardy pedestrian who is willing to walk the 20 kilometres from the railway station to the foot of the Elburz mountains, a trek involving a climb of 310 metres — but only the foolhardy would do so in the summer. Greater Tehran is built at an average altitude of about 1200 metres on a gentle slope running south from the Elburz mountains. The cli-mate has marked seasonal contrasts, with a short spring and autumn separating a long and severely cold winter and a lengthy hot, dry summer. The average tempera-tures in the southern part of the city are 30 °C in July, compared with 23 °C in the northernmost suburbs, and averages of 1 °C and 5 °C respectively in the winter. The northern suburbs get four times (393 mm) the precipitation the southernmost sub-urbs (93 mm) on the fringes of Iran's great central deserts.

Apart from the cold, one of the main drawbacks to the pedestrian in winter is the unmindful way men clear snow off the flat roofs. Coming from four storeys up, a shovel-load of snow and ice is a hazard not to be taken lightly. Summers are torrid, made worse by the rhythm of daily life for many office workers who work for some hours in the morning, go home, and returning in the evening, so creating four peak periods of traffic flow and consequent jams. Some get relief from the heat in the evenings by travelling by bus or car to a park in the north. The orientation of houses also helps: winds tend to blow along the slope, so the most desirable direction for houses is at right angles to the dominant air flow. Suburban roads tend therefore to run east—west between the main traffic arteries going north to south. Traditional Persian houses had wind towers to catch the breeze; modern houses must make do with glass fronts, blinds, and the constant whirr of air conditioners and fans.

Iran is a capitalist society. The Shah is both head of state and ruler. The largest industry however, oil, is state owned, and the state has increasing influence in channelling economic development. Thus, the strength of central government contrasts with Lebanon. Free competition for desirable sites in the city has resulted in clearly defined zones of functional specialization (Bahrambeygui 1972). There is a peak of land values in the central business district, but overall residential land values increase from the south of the city to the north. To start in the southern districts, therefore, is to start in the poorest areas.

Southern Tehran is the reception area for most of the poorer migrants. There are no shanty towns, such as are found in many other very rapidly growing cities. The buildings are of one or two storeys, poorly built and crowded closely together. There are few open spaces for recreation, though the government is trying to remedy this situation. The streets tend to be dirty, the pavements crowded and noisy with the raucous cries of hawkers. The only trees are along the avenues built by Reza Shah during the 1930s. Shops are small and have the range and quality of goods to cater for the low incomes of the population. There are a number of open air vegetable markets, selling produce from all over the country. The south is socially the most conservative part of the city. Here all the women wear *chadors* (a drab garment that shrouds the body from head to toe), and the noise from mosque loudspeakers can be heard everywhere. Alcoholic liquor cannot be bought in any of the shops.

As one goes further north into the limits of the nineteenth-century city and closer to the central business district, the buildings are larger and more imposing, though in the bazaar, which is a warren of streets, everything has a general air of seediness, giving the impression that though there may be fortunes made by the merchants, the really big business is done in the prestige tower blocks at the smart end of the town. Further beyond the bazaar, on the site of a Qajar palace, is a group of ministry buildings – Justice and Finance – where pavement scribes have tables and chairs set out, and, with the typewriters and glasses of tea, sit waiting for illiterates who have forms to fill or letters to write.

Then, along and around Hafez Avenue is a grouping of foreign embassies and department stores. The embassies that acquired their site in the nineteenth century have the largest grounds, since this area was an extra-mural suburb until the present century. The British and Soviet embassies have enormous tree-filled parks, on a scale that befitted British and Russian power in the last century. Beyond this area there is a transition from the city of Reza Shah to modern Tehran. Here is the part of the central business district where are found finance offices, the headquarters of the National Iranian Oil Company, hotels, cinemas and the major airlines' booking bureaux. The services cater for the wealthier foreigners — Danish-pastry shops, super-markets, liquor stores, night clubs and the expensive craft shops for tourists. People wear Western dress.

Up the slope from this district are the beginnings of middle-class Tehran. Land values in the residential areas are lower than further south, though land values along the main roads are very high. The area has mostly four-storey apartment blocks, large houses, immature trees. The building surfaces are white, in contrast to the dun colour of the southern districts. Development in this part of the city after the Second World War tended to follow the two main arteries north to Shemiran, the northernmost district. Later development has filled in the gaps, so that the urban area is now one built up tract stretching from the desert to the mountains. If nineteenth-century, upper-class, central Tehran has the charm of the better parts of many European cities, with its leafy avenues and older buildings, the northern districts look much like a new American city, with super highways that swing out into the desert, tower blocks and glaring sunshine. On the lower foothills of Tochal, the 3 800 m. peak that dominates the northern skyline, are the New University, the Hilton Hotel and the Sheraton Towers block. Those who can afford to live here can indulge in the recreations of the wealthy: skiing in winter at Chalus, or trips to the warm Caspian lowlands. Up here on the hills that overlook the city is the Shah's palace.

# 8. Conclusions

In the foregoing pages we have suggested that in seeking to explain social urbanization, reference must be made to the function or set of functions the city serves. Preindustrial urban development was indigenous in the Middle East, created by local demand rather than by imperial or colonial pressures from outside. The largest and most famous cities had trading contacts through the Old World. But the populations of Istanbul, Cairo, Damascus or Baghdad did not live on spices, jewels or manufactured goods; they were sustained by farming in their agricultural hinterlands. It was, in the last analysis, from the farmers in and around the cities that their real wealth was derived, and it was that which paid for luxuries. Except along the Nile, most cities were located in intensively cultivated nuclei of available water and usable land, separated one from another by sparsely inhabited mountains or desert. Each usually functioned as a central place providing services for the surrounding area. The services could be in the form of craft-manufactured goods or in the form of military security, provided by the garrison.

One such city was Kashan, in central Iran, which was part of a highly organized regional system of settlements maintained by continuous communication between its parts. In this type of Iranian city the social hierarchy in the city-region consisted of an urban-based upper class of officials, carpet manufacturers, landowners, merchants, moneylenders and some clergy, which maintained its economic and social dominance over the illiterate mass of the people through the control of water, land and credit. On a smaller scale a similar social structure was found in the villages, and in many respects it is not easy to distinguish between city and village according to their function, social structure or physical morphology. In a region such as Kashan the carpet owner, the tax gatherer and the moneylender operated alike in city and village, and a large proportion of the 'urban' population was engaged in the 'rural' occupation of farming. Even though in Iran there was an historic tendency not to distinguish between a territory and its principal place, not at least as far as their names were concerned, there is no doubt that the distinction between city and village, and even more between city dweller and nomad, was present in the minds of men.

Life in the preindustrial Middle Eastern city focussed upon a person's family, religion, wider tribal group and their means of getting a living, which in the smaller cities was usually farming. In these respects little distinguished the preindustrial Middle Eastern city from others in the Old World except that it was part of a wider social system, namely the Islamic world, that moulded personal and family relations and also the city's physical form, its mode of government and political structures.

Two aspects of the Islamic city will serve here to illustrate the influence of religion on the shape of society and its continued influence in the present day: government, and the role of the city as cult centre.

Islamic ideology is egalitarian but not essentially democratic. The distinction needs to be emphasized since in Western thought egalitarianism and democracy tend to be confused. To Islam all men are regarded as equal in the sight of God, and no section of society, except perhaps the descendants of Mohammed, could claim privileges that would set them apart from other men; yet the traditional Islamic state was ruled by a small elite concerning itself with maintenance of law and order, the provision of some rudimentary public services and the collecting of taxes to enable them to perform these functions. There were no Islamic corporate city-states, nor was there ever any state practising government by the people. Law and order were preached by orthodox Islamic clergy as the principal civic virtues, perhaps because the alternative of anarchy was suffered too often by too many. The only recognized collective units between the family and the state were ethnic or religious communities. Without any checks and balances within the state, traditional authority tended to be despotic – a tradition that has continued to the present day.

The significance of the city as a cult centre comes from the emphasis on the sacredness of places, in Judaism and Christianity as well as Islam. To the devout Muslim Jerusalem, Mecca and Medina are cities where events took place that were of profoundest significance in the history of the world. Not surprisingly, these cities were and are the foci of intense religious, emotional and political concern. To a lesser extent cities where Islamic saints are buried – the tomb of Imam Reza at Mashad is a good example – are regarded with reverence and are the goal of pilgrimages. At the present time about 900 000 pilgrims visit Mecca every year. The Koran states that every Muslim who can afford to should make the pilgrimage at least once in a lifetime. Administration of the holy places at Jerusalem is once more a bone of contention, nowadays between Arabs and Israelis, as it has been since before the Christian Crusades.

The traditional Islamic Middle Eastern city was transformed by capitalist enterprise, starting in the nineteenth century and, in the twentieth century, by the secular state and rapid population growth. Although the regional centre still functioned as a central place for its surrounding region, the function and limits of the city and its unifying relations with the surrounding region changed as regional self-sufficiency gave way to the demands of an export-orientated economy. In the countryside, communal village or tribal ownership of land was destroyed by the new land market, a market that gave shaikhs the opportunity to usurp rights to the land. Much the same happened in the city, where an urban land market became important for the first time. Wealthier citizens began to build outside the city walls, while within the old city communities based on tribal or ethnic composition lost their collective responsibilities for maintaining order and their functions as taxable units. An example of the changes to secular values that took place as the Islamic framework of urban society was loosened is seen in the codes of conduct laid down for commercial transactions before the twentieth century: business deals in the bazaars of Turkey and Iran were regulated by religiously based codes of ethics to which the merchant could refer, with a religious judge to give advice and rulings in doubtful cases. In modern times the codes have been superseded by government regulations embodying, it is claimed, the original religious principles, but now enforced by the secular authorities.

The comparatively slow changes in the social and physical structure of large cities under the stimuli of economic development and political independence was overtaken by an enormous increase in urban populations, due to natural increase and great numbers of people migrating from the urban hinterlands after the Second World War. Migrants brought with them traditions from their former rural life which were added to the variety of urban life-styles but not immediately absorbed.

People who migrate to the city usually have personal contacts there already, over and above the commercial dealings that link town and country. They may have relatives living there, perhaps settled nomads or villagers who moved before them, and in turn some townsfolk visit the country for recreation, to see relatives, or to escape the heat of the summer. Why people move permanently to the city depends in some cases on the political upheavals that have been normal during the present century, in others on the attractions of town life and work, but above all as far as the mass of migrants is concerned it is a reaction to the inexorable pressure of rural populations on local resources. No longer as vulnerable to disease and disaster as they once were, the peasants of the Middle East are growing rapidly in numbers, but available land and water resources are not growing at the same rate, despite government efforts at rural reform. Once in the city the migrant is likely to move from district to district. Movement over a period of years frequently corresponds to changes in the migrant's financial status. Since to do well in the city implies that the migrant is becoming better versed in the ways of urban life, these residential changes are a sign that social urbanization is taking place.

It should be stressed that natural increase is at least as important as migration in the growth of urban populations in the Middle East – a contrast with other regions, for example sub-Saharan Africa. It follows that except in cities like Amman and Kuwait, which have many young male migrants, the sex-ratio imbalance in Middle Eastern cities is much less than in tropical Africa, and the population is much less transient. The continued subordination of women and the encouragement given to sexuality and fecundity are common to the Muslim world, and the demographic contrasts between city and village in the region are probably less than in other world regions. Urban populations are not therefore composed mostly of first generation migrants. That said, what is there specifically urban about these people living in cities, or what are they acquiring that may be called urban, in the sociological rather than the demographic or geographic sense?

There is a greater concentration of population in what might be described as relatively dense permanent settlements of socially heterogeneous individuals, but there is little sign of the anonymity and alienation which were supposed by some sociologists to be the inevitable result of similar rapid Western urban population growth in the nineteenth century. The Middle East contrasts with nineteenth-century America in having its own established tradition of urban life, and in many of even the largest and more cosmopolitan cities the local core of indigenous inhabitants is preserved. In terms of numbers of people the preindustrial urban tradition is of direct significance in cities with an ancient core, but less where the city has grown so large that the old settlement now forms only a fraction of the total, and least where the colonial influence was strongest or in the many new cities. Added to these indigenes are the migrants who bring with them their traditional ways and persist in them. Also, in all walks of urban life there is much personal contact, and anonymity is hardly a problem, whether among the wealthy whose businesses tend to be known by the name of the family owning them, or among impoverished migrants living with friends or fellow villagers. It is to the state rather than to the city we can assign the role of prime mover in the processes of social change. The city happens to be where those processes are often initiated, though with improved communications between town and country this will be less so in the future.

Religion is a good example of this aspect of social change. Changes in religious habits frequently accompany a move to the city. A man may cease to pray five times a day as he is enjoined, perhaps praying only twice because of the constraints imposed on his time in the city. This is not simply an urban trait, however: nomads and villagers are as likely to neglect some of the prescribed times of prayer. The greatest changes in religious organization have been deliberately implemented by the state rather than caused by population moving from small settlements to larger settlements. Twentieth-century governments have had mixed attitudes to religion but most have curbed the power of religious functionaries. Turkey disestablished religion and supressed institutions of religious learning together with practices associated with but not essential to Islam, such as the veiling of women. Iran by contrast retained the Jafari rite of the Shiite sect of Islam as the official religion, though the veiling of women and other practices have been banned. The ulama were firmly put in their place by Reza Shah, who on one occasion personally took a whip to the ulama in Qom who had made disrespectful remarks about his empress.

There is no one religious standard from which those who move to cities may deviate. Islam contains a wide variety of religious expression, with orthodox schools of law and practice and a deep mystic tradition often associated with heterodox beliefs. The cosmopolitan Cariene has little in common with the puritanical followers of the Wahhabi sect who govern Saudi Arabia. Furthermore, a distinction should be made between sect and religion, particularly in Lebanon where each of the sects is an organized feature of social and political life.

However, there are a number of social changes permeating rural and urban society that are initiated in the town. Women probably suffered more restrictions in the traditional town than in the village; now the reverse is happening. Among migrants the evidence seems to show more tolerant attitudes towards female emancipation after the move to the city. Yet the traditional valuation of family honour has remained remarkably strong, despite the disruptive effects of long-distance moves and wider family connections. In both the old and the new districts of a city like Isfahan many family households are close to relatives, even if not in the same building compound. Traditional social patterns have been well preserved or even reinforced among some migrant groups, as evinced by the tribal Amara migrants in Baghdad, who worked in the city and were thus subject to the rhythms and pressures of urban employment, but whose social, tribal and religious life remained largely untouched by the city. The carry-over of family and tribal traditions from village or desert to the city extends also to personal manners in some places. In Kuwait even callers outside the family circle are hospitably received and entertained in the traditional desert manner, while nearly everywhere in the Middle East greetings are highly stylized, with many enquiries after the health and fortune of individuals and their families and equally formal replies. A visit to an office almost always results in offers of tea, coffee or soft drinks.

Away from the personal level however other aspects of urban society are being altered by the restructuring of the urban economy. Concentration of people in a few national centres is a direct result of the cities' new functions, whereby they have become the chief links between the country, the state, and the wider encompassing system of supranational economic relations, a system which until the Second World War was dominated by the free enterprise, market-directed economies of the West. The new urban functions have operated through the growing corporate sector of the economy, a sector that has been grafted onto the casual street economy and the economy of the bazaar merchants and producer—retailers. The occupational structure of cities reflects the growth of the new sectors and gives some grounds for a class formulation, with upper, middle and lower classes. But here again traditional ideas of status or the claims of education blur the picture, while there are deliberate attempts by Arab socialist governments like Syria and Libya to rub out the picture altogether.

If, as we argue above, the state is now becoming a prime mover in social change, the political complexion of the state will determine the directions of social change. Before dealing with this point further, however, it may help to place Middle East urbanization in a wider context by comparing it with the urban experience of other world regions. Data on physical urbanization are given in the Appendix. It can be seen that in the Middle East physical urbanization is generally at a lower level than Latin America (Brazil for example has 56 per cent of its population in urban areas), but at a higher level than Sub-Saharan Africa, where generally about 15 per cent of the population live in urban areas. The role of the city in Africa differs in emphasis from the Middle East; much of contemporary African urban growth is accounted for by the influx of rural people who come and go between the countryside and the town (Little 1974), and who maintain a stake in the countryside. Neither the city nor the state is primarily responsible for social change but rather the impact of outside economic forces. The 'modern' African town performs functions that are not intrinsic to itself, but originate from the world-wide system of international commercial relations. In consequence cities may barely achieve a civic personality even when as corporations they have a legal and constitutional identity and exercise municipal powers. A similar situation obtains in South Asia and Southeast Asia, though in these regions there has been a long tradition of urban life; here the non-communist countries continue with inherited colonial economic structures, specializing in the production of raw materials for the metropolitan powers. Large cities act as link points between the industrialized countries and their sources of raw materials. Although the proportion of the total population living in urban areas is still comparatively low, the size of the primate cities is extraordinary, with Djakarta and Manila for instance having populations in excess of 6 million. Whether most of these huge Asian urban populations are socially urbanized is doubtful: the cities have been described as being in large measure agglomerations of folk societies and the modernized sector is comparatively small. Even given such disparities between world regions it is widely held that the cities in the Third World represent an identifiably separate type from those of the industrial West or the communist bloc. There is a case for arguing that as cities industrialize they become increasingly alike in many aspects of their social structure, since the increasing complexity of modern technology demands an ever more narrowly defined set of structural imperatives for the city to function. Sociologically the attitudes and beliefs of modern urban man are much the same wherever he is found, and many argue that all modern cities look the same. According to this view, therefore, we are all on roads that converge on similar social forms, with some simply further along the road than others.

There is a counter to this argument:

In all probability we have reached the end of an era of association of (physical and social urbanisation) with western-style industrialisation and socio-economic characteristics. The magnitude alone of some of the urban increments expected in the Third World is such that it will probably become increasingly debatable to what extent this urbanization can be related to very much that is meaningful in past western urban experience (Dwyer 1974: 13).

A similar view is propounded by Berry: the socio-political bases for urban development are so divergent, from conditions of laissez-faire privatism in North America to the highly centralized bureaucratic management of the socialist states, that the human consequences must diverge equally widely. Practically all the divergent types of urban development described by Berry (1973: 178–80) can be found in the Middle East, along with the modes of urban planning associated with each.

Lebanon represents one end of the spectrum of socio-political forms that manage the course of urban development in the Middle East. Lebanon has a free enterprise market economy where economic and political power is vested in the claims of ownership and property, power that is widely dispersed and competitively organized. The result in Hamra of Beirut has been a course of urban development resembling those found in the United States, Canada and Australia, similar to the classical nineteenth-century and early twentieth-century Western urban model, where competition for central urban land has given rising land values and a succession of urban land uses as one land use or social group replaces another. Outside this highly westernized, Americanized district the ethnic and religious groups of Lebanon have retained their identity in separate districts of Beirut. Sunni Muslims, Christians, Shia Muslims and Palestinians tend to live in different districts. Most recently ethnic differences have been exacerbated by the leftward political trend of Palestinians, usually Muslims, as against Phalangist Christian groups. Open bloody street warfare between these groups erupted in 1975, and continued unabated in 1976.

Thus while the growth of a corporate economic sector has encouraged a new middle class, ethnic factors in urban life continue to be reasserted. The wider social consequences of society remaining a mosaic of competing ethnic and capitalist groups can most readily be seen through the physical fabric of Beirut, where the competitive rush for land has ruined one of the most beautiful sites on the Mediterranean shore:

All serenity, all greenery, all scale, all beauty, all urbanity, all civility have been washed aside in the blind and crazy build-up of this pathetic Mediterranean city by the tidal waves of cupidity, caprice, speculation, exploitation and fatalism. Instead of a city fit for humans to live in it has become a big bedroom – a shabby, untidy, unsafe, intimate and dishevelled dormitory – fit for the pleasure seeking, the tourist, the collector of urban revenue (Shiber 1967: 410).

Urban planning follows a tendency to do nothing until problems arise or become so great that some corrective or ameliorative action must be taken to preserve the values of the economy. There are no future, explicit goals, only an implied preservation of the values of the past. In any case agreement on common goals is very difficult, given the differences between the various communities.

To the left of the socio-political form found in Lebanon is the radicalism of the welfare states of Kuwait and Israel, where the free enterprise system is modified by governmental action to reduce social and spatial inequalities. The minimum guarantees for material welfare – medical care, education, employment, pensions and housing – are provided for every citizen, through differential taxation and welfare payments in Israel and the disbursement of oil revenues in Kuwait. The earlier urban planning of both these countries was strongly influenced by the West European, particularly the British, example. The key to successful planning was extensive public ownership of land, allowing Master Planning using zoning ordinances and building regulations and creating highways to accommodate future travel demands. This style of plan is more noticeable in Kuwait, where present trends are predicted into the future, likely problems forecast and appropriate planning measures taken. By constructing a large share of housing in existing towns and by building new towns the public sector is exercising development leadership, leading physical urbanization and social urbanization in new directions.

A more exploitive style of planning can be detected in Iran and, possibly, Turkey. The emphasis here is less on identifying new problems than on seeking out new growth opportunities. Iranian national and urban planning combines entrepreneural, corporate, and private planning, industrial and real-estate development, with the public entrepreneur acting at the behest of private interests. The Shah and the state provide developmental leadership and strategy planning. This is spelt out in the introduction to the Fourth Plan, covering the period March 1968 to March 1973:

in addition to the delegation of more responsibility and authority to local administrative officials, the public itself will have to participate more fully in productive investments and social activities while the efforts of the central government will be directed more to maintaining public order, establishing an infrastructure for economic activity, facilitating private initiative, protecting the rights of the individual, planning, determining overall policies, establishing standards and regulations, coordinating and directing individual endeavours in the national interest (Plan Organization 1968).

Here is a mixture of private interest, public welfare and autocratic rule.

The next step from the state leading in the direction in which urban development should go is commanding it to go there. This requires an explicit set of normative goals based on a desired future, with policies to be designed and plans implemented that guide or force urban development towards those goals. The Arab socialist states, notably Egypt, have tried at times to eliminate free-enterprise competition and with it status differences based on economic rewards, following the socialism of Eastern Europe rather than Western Europe. Cairo now shows a greater uniformity and lack of specialization in the urban fabric than at any time in the last century or the present one, with more highly regimented life-styles and building patterns. Inevitably, to achieve these social goals increasing control and coercive power must be applied by the state and its bureaucracies.

If, to understand (physical and social) urbanisation and its consequences in the mixed economies, one has to understand the nature and resolution of private and public forces, in directed societies one has to understand national goals and the ideologies of the planners, for the most important fact of the past quarter century has been the realisation that such sought after futures can be made to come true (Berry 1974: 171).

Thus the urban ethos developing in the Middle East is compounded of elements of unity and diversity. Its unity comes from the common indigenous origins of urbanism, stamped almost everywhere by the culture of Islam; and, as we have argued in the foregoing chapters, the processes of modern social urbanization do not appear to differ significantly between one part of the region and another; nor does the common experience of new functions being added to the older urban functions. The city now also serves the demands of the modern state. There are many similarities between these demands, whether they are those of the Revolution of the Shah and the People, or the Arab Socialist Revolution. The demography and physical growth of the Middle Eastern cities likewise show a similar range of types through the region, while the balance between natural increase and migration and the relative permanency of migration set the region apart from Latin America or from sub-Saharan Africa. But if the mechanism by which the city transmits the messages of central governments is a common element of unity, the messages are becoming increasingly diverse. Social and physical urbanization in the future will be determined as much by the dissimilar ideologies of individual Middle Eastern states and the planned goals for urban society as by the social, historical and environmental features that Middle Eastern cities have in common.

# Appendix

Total estimated population and per cent of population living in urban areas for selected countries

Data from United Nations Demographic Yearbook 1974

| | Year | Total '000 | Per cent urban |
|---|---|---|---|
| *Middle East and North Africa* | | | |
| Algeria | 1966 | 11 821 | 39 |
| | 1974 | 16 275 | 52 |
| Bahrein | 1972 | 223 | 78.1 |
| Egypt | 1966 | 30 075 | 41.3 |
| | 1974 | 36 417 | 44.3 |
| Iran | 1966 | 25 078 | 25.4 |
| | 1974 | 33 093 | 43.3 |
| Iraq | 1965 | 8 047 | 51.1 |
| | 1974 | 10 765 | 62.6 |
| Israel | 1966 | 2 629 | 81.8 |
| | 1973 | 3 277 | 82.0 |
| Jordan | 1973 | 2 535 | 43.0 |
| Kuwait | 1965 | 467 | 94 |
| Lebanon | 1970 | 2 126 | 60.1 |
| Libya | 1966 | 1 617 | 25.4 |
| | 1974 | 2 240 | 25.8 |
| Morocco | 1966 | 13 323 | 30.5 |
| | 1974 | 16 890 | 37.9 |
| Syria | 1966 | 5 500 | 41 |
| | 1974 | 7 120 | 45.9 |
| Tunisia | 1966 | 4 533 | 40.1 |
| Turkey | 1966 | 32 021 | 34.9 |
| | 1974 | 38 270 | 42.6 |
| *South America* | | | |
| Brazil | 1966 | 83 343 | 51.6 |
| | 1974 | 104 243 | 59.1 |
| Chile | 1970 | 8 853 | 76.0 |
| Columbia | 1966 | 18 620 | 55.5 |
| | 1974 | 23 952 | 64.3 |

| | Year | Total '000 | Per cent urban |
|---|---|---|---|
| Ecuador | 1974 | 6 500 | 41.3 |
| Guyana | 1973 | 757 | 40 |
| Paraguay | 1970 | 2 386 | 35.7 |
| Peru | 1966 | 12 011 | 50.2 |
| | 1974 | 15 382 | 55.3 |
| Venezuela | 1966 | 9 030 | 72.4 |
| | 1970 | 10 398 | 75.7 |
| *Africa* | | | |
| Botswana | 1966 | 524 | 4.5 |
| | 1974 | 661 | 12.3 |
| Burundi | 1965 | 3 210 | 2.2 |
| | 1970 | 3 544 | 2.2 |
| Cameroon | 1970 | 5 836 | 20.3 |
| Central African Republic | 1966 | 1 473 | 26.6 |
| Chad | 1974 | 3 949 | 13.9 |
| Dahomey | 1973 | 2 948 | 13.1 |
| Ethiopia | 1965 | 22 590 | 6.8 |
| | 1974 | 27 239 | 11.3 |
| Gabon | 1970 | 500 | 32 |
| Gambia | 1972 | 383 | 14.2 |
| Ghana | 1974 | 9 607 | 31.4 |
| Kenya | 1969 | 10 942 | 9.9 |
| Liberia | 1971 | 1 571 | 27.6 |
| Madagascar | 1966 | 6 200 | 12.7 |
| | 1970 | 6 750 | 14.1 |
| Malawi | 1966 | 4 039 | 5 |
| Mauritania | 1965 | 1 050 | 6.7 |
| | 1974 | 1 290 | 21.7 |
| Mauritius | 1971 | 822 | 43.9 |
| Nigeria | 1963 | 55 670 | 16.1 |
| Rhodesia | 1966 | 4 620 | 15.9 |
| | 1974 | 6 100 | 19.4 |
| South Africa | 1972 | 22 987 | 47.9 |
| Spanish Sahara | 1974 | 107 | 45.1 |
| Sudan | 1966 | 14 120 | 10.6 |
| | 1974 | 17 324 | 13.2 |

|  | Year | Total '000 | Per cent urban |
|---|---|---|---|
| Swaziland | 1966 | 374 | 7.1 |
|  | 1973 | 463 | 7.9 |
| Tanzania | 1967 | 12 313 | 5.5 |
|  | 1973 | 14 376 | 7.3 |
| Togo | 1974 | 2 170 | 15.2 |
| Uganda | 1972 | 10 461 | 7.1 |
| Zaire | 1966 | 18 287 | 21.6 |
|  | 1974 | 24 222 | 26.4 |
| Zambia | 1969 | 4 056 | 30.4 |
|  | 1973 | 4 635 | 34.3 |

# References cited

Abdel-Latif, A.H. 'The Ecological and Social Structure of Alexandria, Egypt: An Examination of Urban Subarea Data, 1947 and 1960', Unpublished Ph.D. thesis, Ohio State University, 1970.

Abu-Lughod, J. 'Migrant adjustment to city life: the Egyptian case', *American Journal of Sociology* 57 (1961), 22–32.

'Urban–Rural differences as a function of the demographic transition: Egyptian data and an analytical model', *American Journal of Sociology* 69 (1963), 476–90.

'Urbanization in Egypt', *Economic Development and Cultural Change* 13 (1965*a*), 313–43.

'Tale of two cities: the origins of modern Cairo', *Comparative Studies in Society and History* (1965*b*), 429–57.

'Varieties of Urban Experience: Contrast, Coexistence and Coalescence in Cairo' in *Middle Eastern Cities*, ed. I.M. Lapidus, Berkeley and Los Angeles, 1969.

'Rural Migration and Politics in Egypt' in *Rural Politics and Social Change in the Middle East*, ed. R. Antoun & I. Harik, Bloomington, Ind., 1972.

Admiralty. *Handbook for Persia*, London, 1945.

Ajami, I. 'Social classes, family demographic characteristics and mobility in three Iranian villages' *Sociologia Ruralis* 9 (1969), 62–72.

Antoun, R. and Harik, I. *Rural Politics and Social Change in the Middle East*, Bloomington, Ind., 1972.

Ash, J. 'The Progress of New Towns in Israel', *Town Planning Review* 45 (1974), 389.

Aubin, J. 'Elements pour l'etude, des agglomerations urbaines dans l'Iran medieval' in *The Islamic City*, ed. A. Hourani & S. Stern, Oxford, 1970

Azeez, M.M. 'Geographical Aspects of Rural Migration from Amara Province Iraq, 1955–1964', Unpublished Ph.D. thesis, University of Durham, 1968.

Baali, F. 'Agrarian Reform in Iraq: Some Socio-Economic Aspects', *The American Journal of Economics and Sociology* 28 (1969), 61–76.

Baer, G. *Population and Society in the Arab East*, London, 1964.

*Studies in the Social History of Modern Egypt*, Chicago, 1969.

'The Administration, Economic and Social Functions of Turkish Guilds', *International Journal of Middle East Studies* I (1970), 28–50.

Bahrambeygui, H. 'Tehran: An Urban Analysis', Unpublished M.A. Thesis, University of Durham, 1972.

Barth, F. *Principles of Social Organisation in Southern Kurdistan*, Oslo, 1953.

Bartsch, W.H. 'Unemployment in Less Developed Countries: A Case Study of a Poor District of Tehran', *International Development Review* 13 (1971), 19–22.

Beeley, B.W. 'The Turkish Village Coffeehouse as a social institution', *Geographical Review*, 60 (1970).

Berry, B.J.L. *City Size Distributions and Economic Development*, Department of
Geography Research Paper No. 2, Chicago, 1961.
*The Human Consequences of Urbanisation*, London, 1973.
Benedict, P. 'Ula, The Decline of a Regional Centre', Unpublished Ph.D. thesis,
University of Chicago, 1970.
Bharier, J. 'A note on the population of Iran, 1900–1966', *Population Studies* 22
(1968), 273–9.
Blake, G.H. *Misurata: a market town in Tripolitania*, Department of Geography
Research Paper Series No. 9, University of Durham, 1968.
'Israel: immigration and dispersal of population', in *Populations of the Middle
East and North Africa*, ed. J.I. Clarke and W.B. Fisher, London, 1972.
*Marketing in the Misurata region of Libya: tradition and change*, Paper presented
at the Annual Conference of the Institute of British Geographers, Oxford,
1975.
Bourgey, A. and Phares, J. 'Les bidonvilles, de l'agglomeration de Beyrouth', *Revue
de Geographie de Lyon* 48 (1973), 107–39.
Bowen-Jones, H. 'Agriculture', in *The Cambridge History of Iran*, Volume I,
Cambridge, 1968.
Breese, G. *The City in Newly Developing Countries, Readings on Urbanism and
Urbanization*, Englewood Cliffs, New Jersey, 1969.
Byron, R. *The Road to Oxiana*, London, 1950.
Clark, B.D. 'Iran: Changing Population Patterns', in *Populations of the Middle East
and North Africa*, ed. J.I. Clarke & W.B. Fisher, London, 1972.
and Costello, V.F. 'The urban system and social patterns in Iranian cities', *Trans-
actions of the Institute of British Geographers* 59 (1973), 99–128.
Clarke, J.I. *The Iranian City of Shiraz*, Department of Geography Research Papers
Series No. 7, University of Durham, 1963.
'Introduction', in *Populations of the Middle East and North Africa*, ed. J.I.
Clarke & W.B. Fisher, London, 1972.
and Clark, B.D. *Kermanshah: An Iranian Provincial City*, Centre for Middle
Eastern and Islamic Studies, Publication No. I, Department of Geography
Research Paper Series No. 10, University of Durham, 1969.
and Fisher, W.B. (eds.) *Populations of the Middle East and North Africa*,
London, 1972.
Costello, V.F. *Kashan. A city and region of Iran*, London, 1976.
'The Industrial Structure of a Traditional Iranian City', *Tidjschrift voor Econ-
omische en Sociale Geografie* 2 (1973), 108–20.
Darwent, D. 'Urban Growth in Relation to Socio-Economic Development and
Westernisation – A Case Study of the City of Mashad, Iran', Unpublished
Ph.D. thesis, University of Durham, 1965.
Dewdney, J. *Turkey*, London, 1971.
'Turkey: recent population trends', in *Populations of the Middle East and North
Africa*, ed. J.I. Clarke & W.B. Fisher, London, 1972.
'Syria: patterns of population distribution', in *Populations of the Middle East
and North Africa*, ed. J.I. Clarke & W.B. Fisher, London, 1972.
Dodd, P.C. 'Family honour and the forces of change in Arab society', *International
Journal of Middle East Studies* 4 (1973), 40–54.
Dunham, D. 'The courtyard house as a temperature regulator', *The New Scientist*
(1960), 663–6.
Dwyer, D.J. (ed.) *The City in the Third World*, London, 1974.

Elkabir, Y.A. 'The Assimilation of Rural Migrants in Tripoli, Libya', Unpublished
    Ph.D. thesis, Case Western Reserve, 1972.
English, P.W. *City and Village in Iran: Settlement and Economy in the Kirman Basin*,
    London, 1966.
Fathy, H. 'Constancy, Transposition and Change in the Arab City', in *From Medina
    to Metropolis*, ed. L. Carl Brown, Englewood Cliffs, New Jersey, 1973.
Fernea, R.A. 'Land Reform and Ecology in Post-Revolutionary Iraq', *Economic
    Development and Cultural Change* 17 (1969), 356–81.
    'Gaps in the Ethnographic Literature on the Middle Eastern Village: A Classifi-
    catory Exploration', in *Rural Politics and Social Change*, ed. R. Antoun &
    I. Harik, Bloomington, Ind., 1972.
    and Fernea, E.W. 'Iraq', *Focus* 20 (1969).
Ffrench, G.E. & Hill, A.G. *Kuwait: Urban and Medical Ecology*, Heidelberg, 1971.
Fisher. W.B. 'Jordan: a demographic shatter-belt', in *Populations of the Middle East
    and North Africa*, ed. J.I. Clarke & W.B. Fisher, London, 1972.
    'Lebanon: an ecumenical refuge', in *Populations of the Middle East and North
    Africa*, ed. J.I. Clarke & W.B. Fisher, London, 1972.
Floor, W.M. 'The Guilds in Iran – an Overview from the Earliest Beginnings till
    1972', *Zeitschrift der Deutschen Morgenländischen Gesellschaft* 125 (1975),
    99–116.
Gibb, H.A.R. and Bowen, H. *Islamic Society and the West*, London, 1950.
Goitein, S.D. *A Mediterranean Society: The Jewish Community of the Arab World*.
    Vol. I: *Economic Foundations*, Cambridge, Mass., 1967.
    'Cairo: An Islamic City in the Light of the Geniza Documents', in *Middle Eastern
    Cities*, ed. I.M. Lapidus, Berkeley and Los Angeles, 1969.
    *A Mediterranean Society: The Jewish Community of the Arab World*. Vol. II:
    *The Community*, Cambridge, Mass., 1971.
Graber, O. 'The Illustrated Maqamat of the Thirteenth Century: The Bourgeoisie
    and the Arts', in *The Islamic City*, ed. A. Hourani & S. Stern, London, 1970.
Gulick, J. *Tripoli: A Modern Arab City*, Cambridge, Mass., 1967.
    and Gulick, M.E. 'Varieties of Domestic Social Organization in the Iranian City
    of Isfahan', *Annals of the New York Academy of Sciences* 220 (1974), 441–
    69.
Hacker, J.M. *Amman*, Department of Geography Research Papers Series No. 3,
    University of Durham, 1960.
Haggett, P. *Geography: A Modern Synthesis*, New York, 1972.
Halpern, M. 'Egypt and the New Middle Class', *Comparative Studies in Society and
    History* (1967), 97–108.
Hamdan, G. 'The Pattern of Medieval Urbanism in the Arab World', *Geography*
    XLVII (1962), 121–34.
Harik, I.H. 'The Impact of the Domestic Market on Rural–Urban Relations in the
    Middle East', in *Rural Politics and Social Change in the Middle East*, ed. R.
    Antoun and I. Harik, Bloomington, Ind., 1972.
Harrison, R.S. 'Migrants in the city of Tripoli', *Geographical Review* 57 (1967),
    397–423.
Hartley, R.G. 'Libya: Economic development and demographic responses', in
    *Populations of the Middle East and North Africa*, ed. J.I. Clarke & W.B.
    Fisher, London, 1972.
Hasan, M.S. 'Growth and Structure of Iraq's Population, 1867–1947', *Bulletin of
    the Oxford Institute of Statistics* (1958).

Herschlag, Z.Y. *Introduction to the Modern Economic History of the Middle East*, Leiden, 1964.

Hill, A.G. 'Aspects of the Urban Development of Kuwait', Unpublished Ph.D. thesis, University of Durham, 1969.

'The Gulf states: petroleum and population growth', in *Populations of the Middle East and North Africa*, ed. J.I. Clarke & W.B. Fisher, London, 1972.

Hill, M. 'Israel – Planning Machinery', *Built Environment* 3 (1974), 612–16.

Hoselitz, B.F. 'Generative and parasitic cities', *Economic Development and Cultural Change* 3 (1955), 278–94.

Hourani, A. 'The Islamic City in the light of Recent Research', in *The Islamic City*, ed. A. Hourani & S. Stern, London, 1970.

Ibrahim, S.E. 'Urbanization in the Arab World', *Population Bulletin of the United Nations Economic Commission for Western Asia* 7 (1974), 74–124.

Ismail, A.A. 'Origin, ideology and physical patterns of Arab urbanisation', *Ekistics* 195 (1972), 113–23.

Issawi, C. *The Economic History of the Middle East*, Chicago, 1966.

'Economic Change and Urbanization in the Middle East', in *Middle Eastern Cities*, ed. I.M. Lapidus, Berkeley and Los Angeles, 1969.

Jabra, J.I. *Hunters in a Narrow Street*, London, 1960.

Jacobs, N. *The Sociology of Development: Iran as an Asian Case Study*, New York, 1966.

Jones, L. 'Rapid population growth in Baghdad and Amman', *Middle East Journal* 23 (1969), 209–15.

Khalaf, S. and Konstad, P. *Hamra of Beirut. A Case of Rapid Urbanisation*, Leiden, 1973.

Khuri, F.I. 'Sectarian Loyalty Among Rural Migrants in Two Lebanese Suburbs: A Stage Between Family and National Allegiance', in *Rural Politics and Social Change in the Middle East*, ed. R. Antoun & I. Harik, Bloomington, Ind., 1972.

Lambton, A.K.S. *Islamic Society in Persia*, London, 1954.

Lapidus, I.M. *Muslim Cities in the Later Middle Ages*, Cambridge, Mass., 1967.

'Muslim Cities and Islamic Societies', in *Middle East Cities*, ed. I.M. Lapidus, Berkeley and Los Angeles, 1969.

'Muslim Urban Society in Mamluk Syria', in *The Islamic City*, ed. A. Hourani & S. Stern, Oxford, 1970.

Lawless, R.I. 'Iraq: changing population patterns', in *Populations of the Middle East and North Africa*, ed. J.I. Clarke & W.B. Fisher, London, 1972.

Lerner, D. *The Passing of Traditional Society. Modernising the Middle East*, London, 1964.

Levine, N. 'Old Culture – new culture: a study of migrants in Ankara, Turkey', *Social Forces* 51 (1973), 355–68.

Levy, R. *The Social Structure of Islam*, Cambridge, 1962.

Little, Kenneth. *Urbanization as a Social Process*, London, 1974.

Lockhart, L. *Famous Cities of Iran*, Brentford, Middlesex, 1939.

McGregor, R. 'Saudi Arabia: population and the making of a modern state', in *Populations of the Middle East and North Africa*, ed. J.I. Clarke & W.B. Fisher, London, 1972.

Mansur, F. *Bodrum: A Town in the Aegean*, Leiden, 1972.

Morrill, R.L. *Spatial Organization of Society*, Belmont, Calif., 1970.

Mountjoy, A.B. 'Egypt: population and resources', in *Populations of the Middle East and North Africa*, ed. J.I. Clarke & W.B. Fisher, London, 1972.

Nader, L. 'Communication between City and Village in the Modern Middle East', *Human Organisation*, 24 (1965), 18–24.

Petersen, K.K. 'Demographic Conditions and Extended Family Households: Egyptian Data', *Social Forces* (1968), 531–7.

'Villagers in Cairo: Hypotheses versus Data', *American Journal of Sociology* 77 (1971), 560–73.

Plan Organisation, *Fourth National Development Plan, 1968–72*, Tehran, 1968.

de Planhol, X. 'Regional Diversification and Social Structure in North Africa and the Islamic Middle East', in *Rural Politics and Social Change in the Middle East*, ed. R. Antoun & I. Harik, London, 1968.

Porteous, J.D. 'The nature of the company town', *Transactions of the Institute of British Geographers* 51 (1970), 127–42.

Roos, L.L. 'Attitude change and Turkish Modernisation', *Behavioural Science* 13 (1968), 433–44.

Rotblat, H. 'Stability and Change in an Iranian Provincial Bazaar', Unpublished Ph.D. thesis, University of Chicago, 1972.

Sarly, R. 'Israel – Failure of the new towns', *Built Environment* 3 (1974), 612–16.

Saunders, J. *The Muslim World on the Eve of Europe's Expansion*, Englewood Cliffs, New Jersey, 1966.

Scanlon, G.T. 'Housing and Sanitation: Some aspects of Medieval Islamic Public Services', in *The Islamic City*, ed. A. Hourani & S. Stern, London, 1970.

Shiber, S.G. *Recent Arab City Growth*, Kuwait, 1967.

Shorter, F.C. 'Information on fertility, mortality and population growth in Turkey', *Population Index* 34 (1968), 3–21.

Sjoberg, G. *The Preindustrial City Past and Present*, New York, 1960.

Snaiberg, A. 'Rural–urban residence and modernism: a study in Ankara Province, Turkey', *Demography* 7 (1970), 71–85.

Stern, S.M. 'The Constitution of the Islamic City', in *The Islamic City*, ed. A. Hourani & S. Stern, Oxford, 1970.

Thesiger, W. *The Marsh Arabs*, London, 1964.

Turner, J.C.F. *Uncontrolled Urban Settlement: Problems and Policies*, United Nations, New York, 1968.

Van Nieuwenhuijze, C.A.O. *Social Stratification and the Middle East*, Leiden, 1965.

Weber, M. *The City*, New York, 1958.

Wickwar, W.H. 'Pattern and problems of local administration in the Middle East', *The Middle East Journal*, Summer 1958.

Whitehouse, D. 'Excavations at Siraf. Fifth Interim Report', *Iran* X (1972), 63–87.

Yaukey, D. *Fertility Differences in a Modernizing Country*, Princeton, 1961.

# Index